GW01326373

8 Ways of Spending Christmas with Only $10 Creative, Fun, and Meaningful Holiday Ideas on a Tight Budget

Leroy M. Rhoades

Published by MAHAMA MIMI, 2024.

8 WAYS OF SPENDING CHRISTMAS WITH ONLY $10 CREATIVE, FUN, AND MEANINGFUL HOLIDAY IDEAS ON A TIGHT BUDGET

First edition. October 19, 2024.

Copyright © 2024 Leroy M. Rhoades.

ISBN: 979-8227465801

Written by Leroy M. Rhoades.

Also by Leroy M. Rhoades

12 Skills That Will Pay You Forever: Unlocking Timeless Abilities for
Lifelong Success
8 Ways of Spending Christmas with Only $10 Creative, Fun, and
Meaningful Holiday Ideas on a Tight Budget

8 Ways of Spending Christmas with Only $10

Creative, Fun, and Meaningful Holiday Ideas
on a Tight Budget

LEROY M. RHOADES

Table Of Contents

Chapter 1: Planning Ahead for the Holidays

1.1 Budgeting Basics for Christmas

E very year, like clockwork, Christmas rolls around, and with it comes the pressure to spend. Before you know it, you're caught up in the whirlwind of shopping, decorations, travel, and gifts. It's easy to lose control of your finances if you aren't paying attention. But here's the thing—most people never sit down and actually budget for Christmas. They wing it, and when January hits, the bills come crashing in like a tidal wave.

You need a plan, plain and simple. First, look at what you've got. If you've only got $10, that's fine! It's not about how much you have, but how well you manage it. Think about it this way: you wouldn't start a road trip without knowing how much gas is in the tank, right? Same with your Christmas money.

Pull out a notebook or your phone, and write down everything you think you'll need to spend on: gifts, food, maybe a few decorations. Get a sense of where your money is going before you spend a dime. You don't need a complicated spreadsheet, just some basic notes to track your spending.

Once you've got your list, start ranking things in order of importance. If you're only working with $10, you're going to have to cut some stuff. Gifts might have to take a back seat to food, or decorations might not happen at all. The key is to know what's most important to you and focus your money there. Prioritize the experiences and moments that make Christmas special without emptying your pockets.

And let's get one thing straight: do not put Christmas on a credit card. It's tempting, I know. But if you don't have the cash to cover it, you shouldn't be buying it. Putting yourself into debt over a holiday makes no sense. There's nothing magical about January when that credit card bill hits, and suddenly you're scrambling to pay off hundreds of dollars you didn't really have in the first place.

If you're really tight on money, consider setting aside a small amount each week in the months leading up to Christmas. You don't need to save a fortune. Even $1 or $2 a week adds up. By the time December hits, you've built a little holiday fund without feeling the squeeze.

Remember, Christmas isn't a competition. It's not about who can buy the biggest gifts or throw the flashiest parties. It's about celebrating and spending time with people who matter. If you're smart about budgeting, you'll make it through the holidays without wrecking your finances.

1.2 Prioritizing What Matters Most

We often get caught up in the noise of the holiday season. You know what I'm talking about—decorations, gifts, parties, travel plans, all fighting for attention and pulling at your wallet. But if you stop and ask yourself, "What really matters to me during Christmas?" your answer will likely have nothing to do with any of that.

People get so obsessed with making Christmas "perfect" that they forget to ask themselves what they actually want. Is it the fancy gift-wrapping or the smiles from loved ones? Is it the overpriced Christmas tree or spending time with your family? Once you take a moment to prioritize, you'll start to see where you can cut back.

Let's be real here. When you're working with $10, you're going to have to make some choices. You can't have everything. But that's not necessarily a bad thing—it forces you to really think about what makes Christmas special for you. Maybe it's baking cookies with your kids. Maybe it's sitting by the fire with some hot chocolate. These moments cost next to nothing, but they're worth more than any store-bought gift.

Start by making a list of what's most important to you during the holidays. Is it spending time with family? Is it cooking a big Christmas meal? Maybe it's attending a church service or giving back to your community. Whatever it is, make sure your money supports those things first. Don't waste it on things that don't actually add meaning to your holiday.

For a lot of people, gifts are at the top of the list. That's fine—but remember, gifts don't have to be expensive. A heartfelt, handwritten note can mean more than a $50 gift card. Or maybe you spend time making something special for someone, like baking their favorite treat or creating a personalized photo album. It's about the thought, not the price tag.

On the flip side, there are things you'll have to let go of. That might be the fancy wrapping paper or the new Christmas lights you were eyeing. Or maybe it's skipping the big holiday party so you can focus on more personal traditions. Letting go of these extras isn't a failure—it's prioritizing what actually matters.

When you're clear on what's important to you, it's easier to ignore all the noise. You'll feel less pressure to keep up with what everyone else is doing and more confident in your own choices. And in the end, you'll have a holiday season that's not only affordable but also meaningful.

1.3 Setting Expectations with Loved Ones

Here's the thing about Christmas: a lot of the stress comes from expectations. Everyone's got them—whether it's your kids, your spouse, or even yourself. The problem is, if you're not clear about what Christmas is going to look like this year, those expectations can turn into disappointments.

The best way to deal with this? Talk. Have conversations with your family and friends ahead of time about what's realistic. If you're only working with $10, say that upfront. Don't try to hide it or hope no one notices. Be honest about your situation and what you can contribute.

Let's start with your immediate family. If you're cutting back on gifts this year, let them know why. Explain that Christmas is going to be more about experiences and less about stuff. Maybe instead of buying a bunch of presents, you all decide to do something together, like watching a favorite movie, playing a board game, or going for a winter walk. The point is, if they know what to expect, they're less likely to feel let down.

Kids can be a little trickier because they're often bombarded with ads and peer pressure about what Christmas "should" be. But even with them, setting expectations early can make a big difference. Let them know that Christmas isn't all about getting presents. Maybe you have a conversation about what one or two things are most important to them, and you make sure to include that in the holiday. At the same time, be clear that there won't be a mountain of gifts under the tree, and that's okay.

With extended family, setting expectations might involve being upfront about what you can and can't do. If you usually travel for the holidays but can't afford it this year, let them know as soon as possible. Maybe you offer to host a smaller get-together or suggest a virtual holiday party. The key is communication. People might be disappointed, but they'll appreciate your honesty.

This also applies to holiday parties, Secret Santa gift exchanges, or other social events. If you can't afford to participate, don't feel obligated. It's okay to say no, especially if it's going to put a strain on your budget. A simple "I'm keeping things low-key this year, so I'll have to pass" is perfectly acceptable.

And don't forget to set expectations with yourself. We're often our own worst enemies when it comes to holiday stress. You might have a picture in your head of what Christmas is "supposed" to look like, but if that picture doesn't match your reality, you're setting yourself up for frustration. Be kind to yourself and remember that Christmas doesn't have to be perfect. Focus on the things that matter most, and let go of the rest.

In the end, setting clear expectations isn't about lowering the bar—it's about making sure everyone is on the same page. It allows you to have a holiday that's enjoyable and affordable without the pressure of trying to meet unrealistic standards. And trust me, everyone will appreciate that honesty in the long run.

Chapter 2: Creative Gifting on a Shoestring Budget

2.1 DIY Gifts from the Heart

So here we are—Christmas is coming, your wallet's looking thin, and yet, there's still that itch to give. What do you do? You make it work. You turn that small budget into something bigger with heart and hustle. Forget about spending hundreds of dollars on gadgets or wrapping up something shiny from a department store. You're about to get creative—downright resourceful. Gifts don't have to scream expensive to mean something. They just need to come from the right place: you.

DIY gifts aren't just about slapping together some paper and glue, tossing it in a box, and calling it a day. You're putting thought into these gifts—real thought, the kind that reflects how much you care. No two gifts will be the same, and that's the beauty of it. You've got personality, history, stories to tell. You know your people better than anyone, and that gives you a massive advantage.

We're talking about rolling up your sleeves, getting your hands dirty, and bringing your personality right into the picture. There's no hiding behind a price tag. The work, the creativity—that's what matters. If you've got scissors, glue, and a half an idea, you're already halfway there. Sure, it's going to take a bit of time, maybe a little sweat, but it's worth it. And it won't feel like a chore if you lean into it.

A Picture's Worth a Thousand Bucks

First up, photos. You've got am, whether they're stashed in some drawer or piled up on your phone. Use them. People love memories, especially when they're wrapped up in something more personal. Print out some old photos—doesn't have to be fancy, just needs to be meaningful. Slap them in a homemade frame. And no, I'm not talking about going out and buying a frame that costs more than you're willing to spend on groceries.

You can make a frame. Out of what? Well, anything, really. Cardboard, old wood, leftover materials from that project you never finished. Paint it, doodle on it, and write a personal message around the edges— whatever works. You don't need to be Picasso to make something worth hanging. Remember that time you all got drenched in the rain or stayed up all night laughing? Now it's captured, framed, and suddenly, you've made a moment last forever. It didn't cost much, but the impact? Massive.

Homemade Edibles: Good for the Soul, Easy on the Wallet

Then there's the gift of food. There's no need to be a master chef to put together something special. Whip up some homemade goodies—cookies, brownies, or even a batch of grandma's famous fudge. Stick them in a nice jar, tie a bow around it, and just like that, you've made a gift that's not only thoughtful but tasty.

If you're feeling a bit adventurous, make a recipe booklet. Nothing fancy, just a few handwritten pages of your favorite recipes, or recipes that you know they'll love. Maybe there's that one dish you're always asked to make at family gatherings. Share it. Food is connection, and when you make something with your own hands, it goes beyond just filling stomachs—it fills hearts. And don't forget, everyone's gotta eat, right?

The Gift of Time and Skills

Sometimes, the best gift you can give doesn't come in a package at all. Look, you've got skills. Everyone's got something they're good at, whether it's fixing things, organizing, or maybe you're just really great at listening. Offer your time as a gift. Make a little coupon book of "free services" for things you know your loved one could use. Babysitting, yard work, a night of Netflix and pizza with no interruptions—all things that cost you next to nothing but are worth a ton in value.

Got a green thumb? Offer to help them set up a garden. Handy with a wrench? Fix that leaky faucet they've been griping about for months. Time is valuable—more valuable than most people realize. When you give your time, you're showing that you care enough to stop and focus on them.

Personalized Art: No Talent Required

Art doesn't require you to be the next Da Vinci. It's about expression, and the only thing it demands is your effort. Personalized artwork can mean so much. It can be simple, too. Maybe it's a sketch, a doodle, or even some hand-painted design on a piece of wood you found in the garage. Grab some cheap paints, brushes, and let loose. Paint what reminds you of the person—colors, shapes, maybe a quote they live by.

You don't need to overthink it. In fact, don't think too much at all. Just go with it. It's the gesture that counts, and trust me, even the messiest, most abstract piece of art holds a unique charm that a mass-produced print can never have. What's more, your piece can be something they see every day, hanging on their wall or sitting on their shelf. A constant reminder that someone took the time to think of them.

Memory Boxes: Treasure Without the Price

This one's personal. Grab an old shoebox, some wrapping paper, maybe even a few markers. Decorate it however you like—there's no wrong way to do it. Inside? Memories. Notes, letters, small keepsakes that remind them of moments you've shared. You could even toss in some photos, a dried flower from that hike you took last summer, or a ticket stub from a concert you both loved. It doesn't have to be big or flashy—it just needs to remind them of something special.

Fill it with things that matter between the two of you. Write a letter, something heartfelt that they can come back to whenever they want. There's power in words, more than we often realize. This kind of gift doesn't scream money, but it speaks volumes in sentiment.

Knitting, Sewing, and Crafting: Old-School Skills That Pay Off

Got a knack for knitting? Crocheting? Sewing? If you've got even the slightest bit of talent in these areas, put it to use. A handmade scarf, blanket, or even something small like a beanie—these gifts show effort. They're personal, and they take time, which makes them all the more valuable. And let's face it, who doesn't appreciate something that keeps them warm during the winter?

If sewing and knitting aren't your things, don't worry. You can always try your hand at other crafts. Get some beads and make jewelry. String together a bracelet or necklace with their favorite colors, stones, or even their name. It doesn't have to be perfect—imperfections make it real.

Up cycled Gifts: Turning Junk into Treasure

E ver heard the saying, "One man's trash is another man's treasure"? Well, it's true. Take something old, something forgotten, and breathe new life into it. An old chair sitting in your basement? Sand it down, paint it, and suddenly it's a statement piece. Got a bunch of old mason jars? Turn them into candle holders, vases, or storage containers. Up cycling isn't just about being frugal; it's about seeing potential where others don't.

Up cycled gifts come with a sense of accomplishment. You took something that was cast aside and made it meaningful again. That's no small feat. Plus, it's environmentally friendly, and who wouldn't appreciate a gift that's not only thoughtful but also sustainable?

Mix-Tapes (But Make It Modern)

O kay, maybe you're not going to pull out a cassette tape like it's 1990, but the idea of a personalized playlist still holds up. Create a custom playlist of songs that remind you of the person or reflect your shared experiences. Whether it's the song that played during that road trip or the one they couldn't stop singing last year, music is powerful.

Burn it on a CD if they still have a player, or make a digital playlist and share it. Include a note explaining why you picked each song. It's cheap, it's easy, and it's meaningful. Music taps into emotions in a way that few things can.

2.2 Thoughtful Low-Cost Gifts

L et's face it: the myth that thoughtful gifts come with a high price tag needs to be smashed into tiny pieces. You don't have to spend big to make a big impression. People remember gifts because of the meaning behind them, not because of the brand label slapped on the packaging. You can give something cheap, even borderline free, and still make it the most talked-about present of the year. It's all about tapping into what really matters to the person you're giving it to. And it's not that complicated—if you're smart about it, you can craft a low-cost gift that hits all the right notes.

The truth is, anyone can walk into a store, pick something pricey off the shelf, and call it a day. But where's the connection? It's thoughtless. There's no heart in that. The goal here is to look past the price tag and focus on the individual. If you know someone well enough, you can make a gift that makes them pause, smile, and say, "Wow, you actually thought about me." That's the sweet spot.

Let's get into the nitty-gritty. Start with personalization. People love feeling like something was made just for them. You don't need to shell out $500 to monogram a luxury item. Instead, take something simple and make it theirs. Grab a plain mug—cheap as dirt—and give it a facelift. Draw their favorite quote, doodle something that reflects their personality, or write a message that only the two of you would understand. Suddenly, that basic mug isn't so basic. Every time they sip their coffee, they're reminded of the effort you put in. And we're talking a few dollars, maybe less if you've already got some markers or paint lying around.

There's an infinite number of ways to customize a gift without burning a hole in your wallet. Take coasters, notebooks, keychains—you name it. These items cost next to nothing but with a little creativity, they turn into one-of-a-kind pieces. The secret sauce here is effort. People recognize when you put in the time, and it always beats out the flashiest, most expensive gift sitting under the tree.

And hey, don't sleep on handmade cards. Sure, the stores are full of glittery, overpriced Hallmark nonsense, but a card you make yourself? That's a game changer. You don't need to be Picasso. Grab some paper, scissors, glue, maybe a couple of markers, and go wild. Inside jokes, funny doodles, maybe a few words that really speak to your relationship—whether it's a friendship, romance, or family bond. A homemade card cuts through the fluff. It's real, it's personal, and it says exactly what you want it to say. When's the last time someone threw away a heartfelt, handmade card? Exactly.

Then, there's the whole category of gifts that offer experiences over things. People remember experiences. Time spent together or something that enhances their life will always outweigh a material object. Create a "coupon book" filled with things like "a night of movies and popcorn," "a day of help with household chores," or even something as simple as "a walk in the park together." These "services" don't cost you a penny, but they offer something priceless—time and attention. Think about it. You're giving something no one can buy at any store: yourself.

Here's another idea: mix tapes. Okay, not tapes exactly, but the modern equivalent. A curated playlist of songs that remind you of them, that you've shared together, or that you know they'll love. Music connects in ways that objects never can. It sparks memories, emotions, and deep feelings. Create a playlist, give it a creative name, and send it over with a note explaining why you chose each track. It's deeply personal, and it costs nothing but your time. Yet, the impact is massive. Trust me, it'll hit home.

If you're crafty, you can take it to another level with something handmade. No, you don't need to be a DIY master. Think small. Are you good at knitting? Crochet? Whip up a scarf, a hat, or a pair of mittens. Those small, handmade gifts mean someone took the time to make something just for you. It's a personal touch that no store-bought item can compete with. Even if it's not perfect, that's kind of the point. The little imperfections are what make it unique. And the best part? Materials are cheap. You can grab some yarn and knitting needles at a craft store for a few bucks. Time is your only investment here, but that's where the magic happens.

You don't need any special skills to create a thoughtful gift. Take something ordinary and give it new life. Look around your house. You'd be surprised at what you can turn into a meaningful gift. An old picture frame gathering dust in a drawer? Clean it up, maybe give it a fresh coat of paint, and put a photo inside that means something to the two of you. It's not about how fancy it looks; it's about the story behind it. That framed picture isn't just an object—it's a memory. A reminder of a good time. And it cost next to nothing.

Or maybe you've got some old mason jars or small containers just lying around. You could turn those into a DIY spa set by filling them with homemade scrubs, bath salts, or lotions. It's ridiculously easy, costs almost nothing, and yet it feels like a luxury gift. People love pampering themselves, and when you give them something that encourages a bit of self-care, it shows you're thinking about their well-being. Google some basic recipes for scrubs or salts, and you'll see how simple it is to throw this together with stuff you probably already have in your kitchen.

Another way to stretch your dollar is by making "memory boxes." This works especially well for people you've shared a lot of experiences with. Start with an old shoebox or any small container you've got lying around. Wrap it up in some colorful paper or fabric scraps. Fill it with little mementos—notes, pictures, ticket stubs, dried flowers, or anything that represents the memories you've shared together. Maybe even add a letter inside, telling them what these memories mean to you. A memory box is intimate and deeply personal. It's not something you can buy—it's something you create from the experiences only the two of you share. And that's priceless.

Don't overlook the power of repurposing and upcycling. You know that old saying, "One man's trash is another man's treasure"? It's spot on. You've got stuff lying around that, with a little tweaking, can become thoughtful, low-cost gifts. An old chair gathering dust in your garage? Sand it down, repaint it, and suddenly it's a one-of-a-kind piece of furniture. An old shirt that's been sitting in the back of your closet? Turn it into a pillow or a tote bag. You're taking something with no life left in it and breathing new energy into it. Upcycling isn't just thrifty—it's creative, thoughtful, and eco-friendly. People appreciate the effort it takes to give something new life. And bonus points for keeping stuff out of landfills.

One of the easiest ways to create a thoughtful gift is by combining smaller, affordable items into something bigger. Say your friend or family member is a book lover. Don't stress about buying the latest hardcover bestseller—it's probably out of your price range. Instead, put together a small "book lover's kit." Hit up the dollar store for a cute bookmark, grab a paperback classic for cheap, throw in some tea or a candle, and package it all together nicely. You've created a themed gift that shows you've put thought into what they enjoy, and it didn't break the bank.

Gift-giving isn't about flashing cash. It's about effort. It's about showing that you care enough to make something personal. The world has enough generic, one-size-fits-all gifts. What people crave, especially in today's fast-paced, transaction-heavy world, is something that feels like it was made just for them. That's where your focus should be. Forget what society says about expensive presents equating to love or care. You've got everything you need to make this holiday season memorable without breaking the bank. You just have to look beyond the price tag.

2.3 The Gift of Time and Experiences

You know what people don't talk about enough when it comes to gifting? Time. Time is the most valuable resource we have, and it's something you can't buy more of. No one talks about how powerful giving your time can be. It's worth more than anything you can pick up at a store. Think about it: everyone's rushing around, trying to make more money, get more stuff, but in the end, what do people really remember? They remember the moments. The laughs. The shared experiences. That's the stuff that sticks. When you're on a budget, you can't always afford fancy things, but you always have time. The key is learning how to package it right.

Experiences—those are where the magic happens. You can give someone a memory that lasts far longer than any physical gift ever could. And it doesn't need to cost you a thing. We've all gotten presents we forget about within a week, right? Some gadget or piece of clothing that was nice but ended up collecting dust or getting re-gifted. But experiences? They stay with you. They become stories, the kind you tell years later, with a smile or a laugh. That's the power of giving your time and creating moments. You give something that grows in value as the years pass.

Start with something simple. A walk in the park or along the beach. It costs zero dollars, but the conversations you have during that time are priceless. Life moves fast, and sometimes just taking a moment to slow down and spend time with someone is the greatest gift you can offer. You don't need to spend money on fancy outings or expensive dinners to have meaningful experiences. A walk, some fresh air, and a deep conversation—these can be better than anything wrapped up in paper and bows.

And here's the thing about experiences: you can customize them to the person. You know your people. You know what they like to do. Tailor the experience to them, and suddenly, you've taken something that costs nothing and turned it into something they'll never forget. Are they into stargazing? Drive out to the countryside, bring a blanket and a thermos of hot cocoa, and spend a night looking at the stars. Simple, right? But also deeply meaningful. It's quiet. It's intentional. It's you taking time out of your life to be with them in a meaningful way.

Or how about cooking together? Invite them over, pick a recipe you both enjoy (or want to try), and make an event out of it. It doesn't have to be anything gourmet—spaghetti, tacos, a homemade pizza. The act of cooking together, of creating something together, becomes the gift. Sure, the food's a nice bonus, but what they'll remember is the time you spent doing it. The laughs when you mess up the recipe, or the pride when it actually turns out well. That's what sticks with people. And again, the cost? Barely anything.

Another idea: plan a themed movie night. But don't just slap on Netflix and call it a day. Go all out. Pick a theme—like '80s action films, or classic comedies, or maybe a whole franchise like Star Wars. Make a plan, grab some popcorn, and make it an event. You could even print out tickets, make a snack bar at home, or have a themed menu to match the movies. You're giving an experience, not just a night in front of the TV. It feels intentional, and people love that. The cost? Barely anything. The effort? More than a typical gift card, sure, but that's the whole point. You're giving them your time, your effort, and your thoughtfulness. That's what makes it valuable.

Let's talk about the "coupon book." It might sound old-fashioned or even a little cheesy, but done right, it's a killer gift. The key here is in the details. A lazy coupon that says "One Free Hug" isn't going to cut it. What you want is to think about what that person actually needs or would appreciate. Maybe they're stressed out all the time, and what they could use most is a "coupon" for a day of relaxation—where you handle their errands, watch their kids, or take care of whatever small tasks have been nagging them. Or maybe it's a "voucher" for a home-cooked meal on a random weekday when they're too tired to even think about cooking. It's not just the coupons themselves—it's what they represent: you taking the time to help make their life easier.

You want to take it up a notch? Add personal flair to each coupon. Maybe one coupon is for a free "storytime session," where you sit together, pour some drinks, and just share old stories—funny, embarrassing, heartwarming stories from your past. That's something no one else can offer, and it's uniquely yours. If the person you're gifting to has kids, toss in a coupon for free babysitting. It's a gift that lets them take time for themselves, which might be exactly what they need.

Time gifts can also be as simple as offering your skills. Maybe you're handy around the house. Offer to fix something that's been bothering them for ages. A leaky faucet, a squeaky door, or helping them paint that room they've been putting off. Or if you're good with cars, offer a free oil change. If you know your way around a camera, offer to take some photos for them—family portraits, shots for social media, whatever. You're taking something you're already good at and giving them the benefit of that skill, and it costs you nothing but time.

Another thing that works? Sharing knowledge. Maybe you're good at something they've always wanted to learn. Teach them. A cooking lesson, knitting tutorial, or even showing them how to use a piece of software they've been struggling with. Sharing your time to teach them something new is not only thoughtful but also practical. They walk away having learned something useful, and you've created a bond through that shared experience.

One of the most valuable time-related gifts you can give is to help someone achieve a goal. This doesn't have to be some massive, life-altering thing. Maybe they've been talking about wanting to get into running, so offer to be their running buddy for a month. Or maybe they want to get back into reading, so start a book club with them, just the two of you, where you each read a chapter and talk about it over coffee. These small goals that people have—often the hardest part of achieving them is finding the motivation. By giving your time, you're offering that accountability and encouragement they might need to push through.

And then there's travel. Now, I'm not talking about expensive vacations. I'm talking about day trips, local adventures. Most people don't realize how many hidden gems are in their own backyard. Plan a day trip to a nearby city, a national park, a quirky roadside attraction—whatever's within driving distance. Pack some sandwiches, grab a thermos of coffee, and hit the road. You're not just giving them a trip; you're giving them an escape, a break from the routine. It feels spontaneous, even though it's planned. And that's the beauty of it—it feels like an adventure, but it's still easy on your wallet.

And let's not forget that sometimes, just being present is the best gift you can give. In today's world, people are so distracted by their phones, their jobs, their endless to-do lists. A gift of time doesn't always have to be an activity or event. Sometimes it's just sitting down with someone, giving them your full attention, and listening. No distractions. No phones. Just real, undivided attention. You'd be amazed at how rare that is these days—and how appreciated it is. People crave connection, and giving your time in this way shows that you're there for them, fully. It costs you nothing but your presence, but it means everything to the person receiving it.

One of the things people overlook when they're focused on material gifts is the power of spontaneity. It's easy to get caught up in planning and execution, but sometimes the best time-gift is the one that happens on a whim. Call them up out of the blue and say, "Hey, let's go for a drive," or "Let's grab coffee." That unexpected moment when you show up, out of nowhere, to spend time with them—those are the moments people treasure. It's unscripted, unplanned, and purely about the connection between the two of you.

Time doesn't have a price tag. It doesn't come with glitter or wrapping paper. But when you give someone your time, when you give them an experience, you're giving them something far more valuable than anything you could buy. You're giving them a piece of yourself, a memory that'll outlast any object or thing. The power of time and experiences as gifts is unmatched. It's something they'll look back on, years down the line, and think, "That was special." And that's the whole point of gift-giving, isn't it? To create something that sticks with people, long after the moment has passed

Chapter 3: Celebrating with Family & Friends

3.1 Organizing a Potluck Christmas Dinner

You know what makes Christmas dinners amazing? Not just the food. Sure, you've got the mashed potatoes, the turkey, the stuffing—it's all great. But what really makes the meal special is the people around the table. The laughter, the stories, the shared moments—that's the secret sauce. And if you want to throw a memorable Christmas dinner without spending a fortune, potluck is the way to go. It's not only budget-friendly, but it also brings everyone together in a way no catered, restaurant-style dinner ever could.

Now, let's not kid ourselves—throwing a big Christmas dinner can get expensive fast. But here's the beauty of a potluck: the costs get spread out, and no one person is stuck footing the whole bill. You're pooling your resources. Think about it like this—everyone's got that one dish they make really well. Whether it's Aunt Linda's sweet potato casserole or your friend's to-die-for mac and cheese, everyone has something they're proud to bring. When people contribute, it's not just about the food, either—it's about feeling involved. It's about saying, "I'm a part of this. I helped make this night happen."

So, how do you pull off a killer potluck Christmas dinner? First, you've got to be the ringleader. You need to organize, but without making it feel like a chore for anyone. People don't want to feel pressured into bringing food. They want to feel excited about it. That starts with getting the invites out early. The moment you decide you're doing a potluck, let people know. Give them plenty of time to plan. The worst thing you can do is spring it on them last-minute and expect them to come up with something great. That's how you end up with five people bringing a bag of chips and one person awkwardly carrying a tray of brownies that aren't even cut yet.

Once you've got your crew, the next step is coordination. You don't need to micromanage (nobody wants that), but you've got to make sure you're not ending up with twelve desserts and no mains. That's where a sign-up sheet or a simple group text comes in. Give people options. Have categories: appetizers, mains, sides, desserts, drinks. Let them pick what they want to bring, but keep an eye on it so you can nudge someone to switch if the balance is off. The key is to be flexible but keep things under control. No one wants to show up to a potluck and find out they're the seventh person to bring a green bean casserole.

Now, a pro tip: encourage people to make what they're good at. This isn't the time to try out some crazy new recipe they saw on YouTube. This is about comfort food, family classics, and dishes they know will hit the mark. When people bring their A-game, it raises the whole event. Everyone loves the feeling of pride when people rave about their dish. And let's face it, people want to show off a little. It's Christmas. It's family and friends. Let them bring the dish they're known for and let them bask in the compliments. That's part of the fun.

And while we're on the topic of fun—don't stress too much about the presentation. You're not hosting a five-star dinner party with white-glove service. Potlucks are meant to be casual. You don't need matching serving dishes or perfectly coordinated table settings. In fact, the mix of different styles, dishes, and serving ware adds to the charm. It's the ultimate "come as you are" meal. Some people will bring their dish in a fancy casserole dish, others might show up with something in a Tupperware. It doesn't matter. What matters is the food and the people sharing it.

But here's the part a lot of people forget about when planning a potluck: you're still the host. Even though everyone's bringing something, you've got to make sure the space is set up for success. Make sure there's plenty of room for people to set their dishes down, and think about the flow of the room. You don't want everyone crowding around one tiny table, juggling plates and elbows. Spread things out. Set up stations if you can. Drinks in one area, appetizers in another, mains somewhere central, and desserts off to the side so people can graze without bumping into each other. A little pre-planning on your part makes the whole thing feel smoother and more relaxed.

Oh, and here's a trick: have some backup essentials on hand. Even with the best-laid plans, someone's bound to forget something. They'll show up without serving spoons, or they'll realize they didn't bring enough drinks. Be ready for that. Stock up on the basics—extra napkins, utensils, cups, maybe even some simple side dishes like a salad or bread that you can pull out if needed. It's all about being prepared without being over the top.

And about those drinks—don't overcomplicate it. You don't need a full bar or fifty different types of beverages. Stick to a couple of crowd-pleasers. Maybe a signature punch (alcoholic or non-alcoholic) that you can make in a big batch, plus some water and soda for the non-drinkers. If people want something special, they can bring their own, but you're providing the basics. Keep it simple. The focus is on the meal and the company, not on who's got the fanciest cocktail.

The other part of hosting a potluck that's often overlooked is setting the mood. You don't need a lot of decorations, but you do need the right vibe. Christmas is already a time when people feel nostalgic and connected, so lean into that. Put on some music—classic Christmas songs, soft background tunes that get people feeling festive. Light a few candles, turn down the harsh overhead lights, and let the glow of the Christmas tree (if you've got one) set the tone. It's all about creating an atmosphere where people can relax and enjoy themselves. You want your space to feel warm and inviting, not overly staged or stiff.

And let's talk about what happens after the meal. A potluck isn't just about eating—it's about the whole experience. Don't let things fizzle out once the plates are cleared. Plan a little something for afterward. Maybe it's a game everyone can play, like a round of charades or a Christmas trivia contest. Maybe it's just sitting around the table, swapping stories, or watching a Christmas movie together. The key is to keep the energy going. Potlucks are about community, about spending time together, so extend that connection beyond the food.

Now, one thing you're going to need to be ready for is leftovers. And at a potluck, there will always be leftovers. That's just the nature of the beast when everyone brings a big dish. Make it easy for people to take some food home—stock up on some cheap containers or ask everyone to bring their own. No one wants to lug home their half-eaten casserole in the same dish they brought it in. Plus, sharing the leftovers is part of the fun—it's like a little bonus gift at the end of the night. Everyone leaves with something to enjoy later, and it keeps that Christmas spirit going even after the party's over.

Potlucks aren't just about saving money. Sure, they're budget-friendly, but they're also about sharing. They're about connection, collaboration, and letting everyone feel like they're contributing. When people bring food to the table—literally and figuratively—it deepens the bonds between them. It's not just you, the host, doing all the heavy lifting. It's a team effort. And that's what makes the whole experience richer. You're sharing more than just a meal—you're sharing a moment, a memory.

And at the end of the day, that's what Christmas is about, right? It's about coming together, spending time with the people you care about, and creating memories that will last long after the food is gone. So, don't stress about having the perfect dinner or the fanciest setup. Focus on the people, the shared laughter, the stories. Let the potluck take the pressure off you as the host and turn the night into a true collaboration of friends and family.

3.2 Hosting a Fun Game Night

———

When it comes to bringing people together, nothing beats a good old-fashioned game night. I'm not talking about sitting around, staring at your phones, or awkward small talk. I mean full-on, everyone-laughing-so-hard-they-can't-breathe, competitive, edge-of-your-seat fun. And you know what? Hosting a game night doesn't cost much, but it's one of the most effective ways to bond with family and friends. No need for fancy plans or expensive trips—just a few games, some snacks, and the right vibe. That's all it takes to turn an average evening into something people will be talking about for months.

Here's the thing: people crave connection, especially during the holidays. We're all busy with work, deadlines, and life in general. So, when you host a game night, you're offering a chance for everyone to cut loose, be themselves, and just have fun. It's a break from the routine. But don't just throw a random game out there and expect everyone to fall in love with it. You've got to plan it right. You've got to know your audience.

Start by picking the right games. That's where a lot of people go wrong—they think any game will do. But the key to a successful game night is choosing games that match the crowd. You can't expect a group of hardcore Monopoly fans to get into a trivia night, or vice versa. And you definitely don't want to pick something too complicated if you've got a mixed crowd. The best games are easy to learn, fast-paced, and—most importantly—fun. We're talking games that everyone can get involved in, even if they've never played before. Card games, charades, trivia—stuff that doesn't need a huge setup or deep strategy. Keep it light. Keep it fun.

Here's a tip: kick things off with an icebreaker game, something simple that gets everyone laughing and comfortable. Maybe it's a game of Pictionary where people have to draw ridiculous things, or a round of "Two Truths and a Lie." These are games that let people loosen up before diving into more competitive stuff. The goal at the start isn't to win—it's to get people in the right headspace. You want everyone to feel like they're part of the action, not just sitting on the sidelines, unsure of what to do.

And let's talk about atmosphere. You've got to set the stage. You can't just toss a deck of cards on the table and expect magic to happen. You need to create an environment that says, "We're here to have fun." That means lighting, music, snacks—everything should be geared toward making the night feel special. But don't overthink it. You don't need to rent out a hall or hire a DJ. Dim the lights a bit, throw on some background music—nothing too loud, just enough to set the mood—and make sure people are comfortable. Scatter some pillows around the floor, clear out some space for the games. Let it feel casual, but intentional.

Snacks are essential. I can't stress this enough. You've got to have finger food, something people can grab without stopping the action. You don't want a formal sit-down meal—this is game night, not a dinner party. Think chips, popcorn, dips, maybe a few cookies or brownies. And keep the drinks simple. A few bottles of soda, maybe some beer or wine if that's your thing, but keep it relaxed. The focus should be on the games, not the catering.

Now, once everyone's warmed up and ready, that's when you can bring out the big guns. This is when you pull out the games that get people talking smack, laughing hysterically, or going all in for the win. Games like "Cards Against Humanity," or "Apples to Apples" work for large groups because they're ridiculous, and they keep the energy up. Or, if you're looking for something with a little more strategy, maybe bust out "Catan" or "Ticket to Ride." Just remember, the longer a game takes, the more you risk losing people's attention. So, unless you know your group is down for it, stick with games that have a quicker pace.

And here's the secret sauce for game night success: make it competitive, but not cutthroat. You want people invested, but you don't want it to turn into a bloodbath. Keep the competition lighthearted. Maybe offer small prizes for the winners—nothing fancy, maybe just a silly trophy or a homemade certificate that says "Game Night Champion." People love the idea of winning something, even if it's just for bragging rights. But make sure everyone's having fun. If you sense that someone's getting frustrated or too competitive, steer the group back toward something lighter.

Don't underestimate the power of team games either. Games like charades or "Heads Up!" are awesome because they force people to work together, and they're usually pretty hilarious. Plus, team games help break up any cliques that might form during the night. You don't want the same group of people hanging out in the corner while everyone else is trying to get in on the action. Mixing people up keeps things fresh and ensures everyone feels included.

And here's where things get really fun: the more ridiculous, the better. People come alive when the games are a little silly. A game like "Twister" might seem like something from your childhood, but trust me, when adults get involved, it's hysterical. Or how about a scavenger hunt around the house? People don't expect it, but it gets them up, moving, and thinking outside the box. It's unexpected, and that's what makes it memorable. You're not just playing games; you're creating moments that will have people laughing long after the night's over.

One thing you've got to remember: not everyone is going to want to play every game. That's okay. Don't force it. If someone's more into watching or just wants to sit out a round, let them. The worst thing you can do is make people feel like they have to participate. Game night is about fun, not pressure. If someone's having a blast just watching the chaos unfold, that's a win too.

At some point, someone's going to get ultra-competitive. It's inevitable. You're going to have that one person who takes winning a little too seriously. That's where you, as the host, have to step in and keep the vibe light. Crack a joke, move the game along, or even take a break if you need to. No one wants to feel like the night is getting too intense. The goal is laughter, not stress.

And don't forget to mix up the games as the night goes on. Maybe start with something simple and then build to more complex games. By the time people have had a few snacks and loosened up, they'll be ready to dive into something with more strategy or skill. But keep an eye on the energy in the room. If things start to lag, bring back a quick, fun game to pick up the pace again. The key is to keep things dynamic and keep people engaged.

One thing that really elevates a game night is a little friendly smack talk. Nothing over-the-top, but a little teasing can go a long way in building the energy in the room. Encourage it. Let people roast each other a bit, make it competitive in a fun way. If someone pulls off an awesome move or wins a round in spectacular fashion, give them a moment to gloat—but then bring it back to the group. The goal is to make sure everyone's involved and having a blast.

And if you really want to take it to the next level, make it a themed game night. Maybe it's "80s Night" and everyone dresses up, or "Superhero Night" where people come as their favorite characters. Adding a theme gives the whole night a layer of creativity and gets people even more invested. Plus, it makes for great photos and memories. Themed nights don't have to be expensive or elaborate—just a little something extra to make the night stand out.

One thing's for sure: you've got to know when to call it a night. Don't drag it out. End on a high note. If you notice people getting tired or the energy dipping, wrap it up before the fun fizzles out. You want people leaving with a smile, not feeling like they're stuck in a never-ending marathon of games. Trust your gut on this one. It's better to end the night with everyone still laughing and having fun than to push through and lose the momentum.

In the end, hosting a game night isn't about being fancy or elaborate. It's about creating a space where people can let loose, have fun, and enjoy each other's company. It's about laughter, connection, and a little healthy competition. So, don't stress the details. Pick the right games, set the mood, and let the fun unfold naturally. When you get it right, game night isn't just a get-together—it's an event. It's something people will look forward to every time, something they'll remember, not because of the games themselves, but because of the shared experience. And that's what it's all about: bringing people together for a night they won't forget.

3.3 Making the Most of Virtual Gatherings

The world has changed, and let's be real—virtual gatherings aren't going anywhere. We've all learned how to adapt to a screen instead of a living room, but just because we're not face-to-face doesn't mean we can't still have a great time. Sure, you're not passing around appetizers or giving out hugs when someone walks through the door, but that doesn't mean a virtual gathering can't be full of laughter, connection, and celebration. You just have to approach it with the right mindset. If you think a Zoom call is going to be dull, then yeah, it will be. But if you treat it like the real deal, that energy will spill over and take everyone with it.

First off, let's talk about mindset. The biggest mistake people make with virtual gatherings is treating them like a chore. You've probably been on those calls where everyone's staring at the screen, waiting for something to happen, feeling awkward, and checking their phone when they think no one's looking. But the moment you stop treating it like a second-rate get-together, everything changes. Treat it like a real event. If you were hosting people at your house, you wouldn't just throw them in a room and say, "Alright, entertain yourselves." You'd plan. You'd think about how to get everyone involved. That's exactly what you need to do here. Virtual doesn't mean half-assed.

The beauty of virtual gatherings is that distance means nothing. You can connect with people from across the country, across the globe. That friend who moved to Australia? They're suddenly part of your holiday celebration again. Grandma who lives two states away? She's right there, sharing stories like she's at the table with you. Take advantage of that. Don't just think of virtual as a compromise. Think of it as an opportunity to bring people together who normally wouldn't make it.

Now, the first thing you've got to handle is the tech. Yeah, I know, it's the boring part, but you need to get it out of the way. Don't wait until five minutes before the party to figure out your video conferencing platform. Whether it's Zoom, Google Meet, or even FaceTime, test it ahead of time. Make sure you know how to share your screen, mute people, and deal with any connection issues that might pop up. Have a plan for the inevitable "I can't hear you" or "You're frozen" moments. The smoother the tech side goes, the more you can focus on having fun.

And speaking of fun, don't fall into the trap of just sitting there and talking. That works for a while, but it's going to fizzle out fast. People need structure, especially online. Plan activities, just like you would for an in-person party. Games are your friend. There are tons of online options—virtual charades, trivia, even Pictionary if you're feeling creative. You can use apps like Jackbox, or even something simple like a good old-fashioned scavenger hunt where people have to run around their house to find items. It's silly, but it works. The key is interaction. You want to keep people engaged, not just staring blankly at the screen.

Another thing: just because you're on a screen doesn't mean you can't set the vibe. Think about your background. Seriously. We've all seen those calls where someone's sitting in front of a messy kitchen or a blank wall, and it just kills the mood. Set up in front of your Christmas tree, or hang some lights, or even use a virtual background if you've got to. You're setting the tone. If you're festive, it'll encourage everyone else to get into the spirit too. You wouldn't host a Christmas party in a room with bare walls, right? So, bring that same energy to your virtual setup.

Don't forget the music. Even though everyone's in different places, music can still bring the whole group together. You can create a shared playlist on Spotify and let everyone add their favorite holiday tunes. Or, better yet, play DJ for the night. Keep the music playing softly in the background during lulls, or crank it up between activities to keep the energy going. It's little touches like this that make a virtual gathering feel like a real party, not just another work meeting on Zoom.

And here's a pro tip: plan for food and drinks. Just because you're not all together doesn't mean you can't share a meal—or at least the spirit of one. How about everyone makes the same recipe beforehand, then you all sit down and eat together? Or maybe it's a cocktail night where everyone mixes up their favorite drinks and toasts on screen. You can even send out a list of ingredients ahead of time, so everyone's on the same page. If you want to get really creative, have a virtual cooking session where everyone prepares the same dish in real time. It's messy, it's chaotic, but it's a ton of fun, and it gives everyone a shared experience.

Now, one of the big challenges with virtual gatherings is making sure everyone gets to talk. In a real party, conversations flow naturally, people break off into smaller groups, and you can bounce around from one person to another. Online, that's trickier. If everyone tries to talk at once, it's chaos. But if no one talks, it's awkward. So, you've got to find a balance. Break things up into smaller groups for part of the night. You can do this with breakout rooms on Zoom or by rotating people through different calls. It lets people have those more intimate conversations that are hard to do with 15 people on one screen. Just make sure to mix up the groups so everyone gets a chance to chat.

One thing that can make or break a virtual gathering is how you handle surprises. In person, surprises happen naturally—someone shows up with a gift, or there's a funny moment that everyone laughs about. Virtually, you've got to create those moments. Plan for surprises. Maybe it's a surprise guest—someone everyone hasn't seen in a while who pops into the call. Or maybe it's a virtual Secret Santa where everyone opens their gifts on screen. The point is, keep people on their toes. Don't let the night get predictable. Virtual doesn't have to mean boring.

And let's talk about gifts for a second. Opening gifts on a video call might sound weird, but it works. In fact, it can be even more special. You get to see everyone's reactions, you get to share the moment in real time, and it makes the whole gift-giving experience feel a little more connected. Just make sure people open their gifts one at a time, or else it's going to turn into a jumble of noise and confusion. And if you really want to up the ante, send out little party favor boxes ahead of time. Nothing fancy—just something small that everyone can open during the gathering. It's those little touches that make people feel like they're part of something special, even from a distance.

Let's not forget the emotional part of this. Virtual gatherings, especially around the holidays, can stir up feelings. People might be missing loved ones or feeling isolated, and that's okay. Don't shy away from it. Lean into it. Create space for people to share what's on their minds. Maybe open the floor for people to talk about their favorite holiday memories or traditions. Let the conversation flow naturally, and don't rush it. One of the benefits of virtual gatherings is that people feel a little more comfortable opening up—there's a safety in the distance. Use that to your advantage. Let people connect on a deeper level.

Another great way to create shared experiences is to plan a virtual movie night. Pick a holiday classic, sync up your start times, and hit play. Platforms like Netflix Party make it easy to watch together and chat while the movie plays. It's not about the movie itself—it's about laughing at the same parts, making jokes, and feeling like you're all sitting on the same couch, even though you're miles apart. You can even turn it into a drinking game or a bingo night if you want to add a little more excitement.

Now, let's get practical for a second. Virtual gatherings have a time limit. People can only stare at a screen for so long before they start to fade. So, keep things moving. Have a loose agenda—games, activities, conversation topics—but don't let it drag on forever. You want people to leave the call feeling energized, not drained. And hey, if people want to stick around and chat after the official "end," great. But you've got to know when to call it. Don't be afraid to wrap things up on a high note.

One thing that can elevate a virtual gathering is using it as an opportunity to give back. Maybe you all chip in for a charity donation, or you organize a virtual volunteer event. It doesn't have to be big or complicated—just something that reminds everyone what the holidays are really about. Even if it's as simple as each person sharing how they plan to help someone this season, it adds a layer of meaning to the gathering.

Finally, here's the most important thing: don't treat a virtual gathering like a consolation prize. This isn't "well, we can't be together, so I guess this will do." No. This is a real celebration. It's a real connection. The medium doesn't matter—it's the people who matter. If you go into it with the attitude that this is going to be awesome, that energy will carry through the screen. People will feel it. They'll engage, they'll laugh, and they'll leave feeling like they were part of something special.

Virtual gatherings might not be traditional, but they can be just as meaningful—if not more so—because they force you to focus on what really matters: the people you're sharing the time with. So, plan it out, set the mood, keep the energy up, and watch how even a video call can turn into a night everyone will remember.

Chapter 4: Holiday Fun Without Breaking the Bank

4.1 Free or Inexpensive Holiday Activities

Let's cut to the chase—holiday fun doesn't have to come with a giant price tag. You don't need to blow your budget to make memories that last a lifetime. People tend to get swept up in the idea that more money means more joy, but that's a trap. It's not the fancy presents, the elaborate parties, or the over-the-top vacations that make the season special. It's the little moments, the shared experiences, the time spent together. And guess what? Most of those things don't cost much, if anything at all.

Think about it: what do you remember from holidays past? The glitzy decorations? The expensive gift you got that one year? Or was it the laughter during a snowball fight, the warmth of a fireplace, or the smell of cookies baking in the oven? I'm betting it's the latter. So let's focus on that. You can fill your holidays with incredible moments without emptying your wallet. You just need to get creative and shift your mindset.

First on the list: go outside. Nature's free, and it's spectacular during the holidays. Depending on where you live, winter might bring snow, crisp air, or a simple change in the landscape, but whatever it is, embrace it. Bundle up and take a walk. Look at the Christmas lights in your neighborhood. There's something about seeing all those houses lit up, each one different, each one telling its own little story. People put so much effort into their displays—why not enjoy it? Make it a game: vote on the best-lit house, the most over-the-top display, the one that feels the most "classic Christmas." It's simple, but it gets everyone in the holiday spirit.

Speaking of lights, don't underestimate how magical a free light display can be. Plenty of cities and towns put on light shows for the public, and they're usually free or dirt cheap. Pile into the car with some blankets and hot chocolate, blast your favorite holiday music, and take a tour of the best spots. There's something about seeing twinkling lights in the cold that just brings a sense of wonder, no matter how old you are.

And if you're lucky enough to have snow, well, that's a playground waiting for you. Build a snowman, have a snowball fight, or if you want to get really ambitious, make a snow fort. The best part? It's free entertainment. Sure, it's cold, and you'll probably get wet, but that's all part of the fun. It's one of those rare moments when adults get to act like kids again. And kids? They're in their element. No one ever says, "I wish I hadn't gone outside to play in the snow." It's the kind of fun that costs nothing but leaves you feeling alive, connected, and genuinely happy.

And let's talk about ice skating. A lot of towns set up public rinks during the holiday season, and they're often either free or really cheap. You don't need to be a pro skater to enjoy it. In fact, the less graceful you are, the more fun it tends to be. Slipping and sliding all over the ice, laughing as you try not to fall—it's one of those activities that's all about the experience, not perfection. Grab a group of friends or family and hit the rink for an hour or two. It's an inexpensive way to make memories, and it gets everyone moving, which is always a bonus when you're stuffed full of holiday treats.

Now, maybe you're more of an indoors person, or the weather's not playing nice. That's fine. The holidays offer plenty of low-cost indoor activities too. Take movie nights, for instance. This one's a classic, but it works. Queue up your favorite holiday movies—whether you're into the old-school stuff like It's a Wonderful Life or more modern hits like Elf—and make a night of it. You don't need a fancy theater or high-tech equipment. Just dim the lights, pop some popcorn, grab some blankets, and you're good to go. The key here is to make it special. Maybe have everyone vote on the movie, or turn it into a marathon where you watch a few back-to-back. It's about creating a cozy atmosphere where everyone can relax and enjoy the magic of the season without spending a dime.

And don't forget about baking. Holiday baking isn't just about the end result—it's the process. It's the smell of cookies in the oven, the mess of flour on the counters, the fun of decorating sugar cookies with way too many sprinkles. Baking is one of those activities that brings people together. Get the kids involved, or invite friends over for a cookie-decorating party. It's low-cost and hands-on, and at the end, you've got delicious treats to share. You don't need to be a master baker. Even a simple batch of cookies becomes special when you're making them together.

And while we're on the topic of togetherness, don't forget about crafting. Whether it's homemade ornaments, cards, or decorations, crafting is another inexpensive way to spend time with loved ones. Hit up your local dollar store for supplies, and then spend an afternoon creating something. It doesn't have to be Pinterest-perfect—it just has to be fun. And when it's all done, you've got something tangible to remind you of the time you spent together. Plus, if you're into giving gifts that feel personal, homemade crafts make great presents.

Here's another idea that costs next to nothing: storytelling. Gather everyone around the fireplace (or, if you don't have one, just dim the lights for that cozy vibe) and take turns sharing holiday stories. They can be personal memories, made-up tales, or even reading from a favorite holiday book. It might sound old-fashioned, but there's something special about storytelling that taps into the very heart of the holiday season. It's about slowing down, listening, and sharing moments that don't involve screens or gadgets. And if you've got kids, this can be a magical experience for them—they'll remember these moments far more than any toy they unwrapped.

You can also create your own traditions. Not everything has to come from a store or a guidebook. Start something new that doesn't cost a thing. Maybe it's a family walk on Christmas Eve, or maybe you all gather around to write down your wishes for the new year and share them with each other. It's about finding ways to connect, to make the season feel special in a way that's uniquely yours.

One tradition that doesn't cost much but has a huge impact is volunteering. The holidays are a great time to give back, and doing so as a family or with friends adds meaning to the season. Whether it's serving meals at a local shelter, collecting coats for the homeless, or simply shoveling a neighbor's driveway, acts of kindness remind us that the holidays aren't just about receiving—they're about giving. And the best part? Giving back costs nothing but your time and effort, yet it fills you up in a way that no store-bought gift ever could.

And if you're looking for a little more excitement without the expense, keep an eye out for free holiday events in your community. There are often tree lighting ceremonies, holiday parades, or free concerts that bring the whole town together. These events capture the holiday spirit and give you a sense of community that's hard to replicate in other ways. Plus, they're a chance to get out of the house and enjoy the season without spending a fortune.

Another fun, low-cost idea? A holiday photo scavenger hunt. Make a list of things to find around town—decorated trees, a snowman, holiday lights, someone dressed as Santa—and see who can snap the most photos. It's a great way to get out, explore your community, and have a little competitive fun with friends or family. And the best part is, at the end of the hunt, you've got a bunch of great holiday photos to look back on.

And finally, don't overlook the power of just being present. It sounds simple, but in a world that's always go-go-go, taking time to be fully present with the people you care about is a gift in itself. You don't need a fancy party, an elaborate event, or expensive gifts to make the holidays meaningful. Sometimes, the best thing you can do is slow down, put away the distractions, and just enjoy the company of the people around you. Whether that's a quiet night at home, a shared meal, or a walk through the neighborhood, those moments of connection are what make the holidays special. And they don't cost a thing.

So this holiday season, ditch the idea that fun has to come with a price tag. Focus on the things that matter: spending time together, creating new memories, and enjoying the little things that make the season magical. Whether you're outside in the snow, huddled up watching movies, or baking cookies with loved ones, remember that the best holiday moments are often the ones that don't cost a thing.

4.2 Exploring Christmas Light Displays

There's something magical about Christmas lights. It doesn't matter how old you are or how many times you've seen them. When the streets come alive with twinkling displays, everything feels different. The air feels crisp, and suddenly, it's like you're walking in a scene from a movie. And guess what? This holiday magic doesn't cost much. In fact, exploring Christmas light displays is one of the best ways to soak in the holiday spirit without spending a fortune. You don't need to shell out hundreds of dollars on expensive events when some of the most breathtaking displays are free for the taking.

Let's get one thing straight: the power of Christmas lights isn't just about brightness or scale. Sure, a massive tree covered in tens of thousands of lights will catch your attention, but sometimes the most meaningful displays are found on quiet streets, with a single strand of lights around the door or a few well-placed bulbs illuminating a snow-covered front yard. That's the beauty of it. Each display has its own story to tell, and all you need to do is look.

The trick is to make a night of it. Don't just hop in the car and drive aimlessly around the neighborhood. Plan it out. Think of it like a treasure hunt, with Christmas lights being your treasure. Start by mapping out neighborhoods or areas known for their festive displays. Many towns even have entire streets or blocks where the houses compete to outshine one another. That's where the magic happens. You drive down the street, and it's like being transported to a whole different world. Houses lit up from top to bottom, inflatable snowmen towering in the yard, reindeer seemingly leaping off rooftops, and of course, the occasional "Clark Griswold" house that's so over-the-top you can't help but stop and stare.

But don't make it a rushed thing. Slow down, take your time. Roll down the windows if the weather allows, let the cold air in, and blast some Christmas music. This isn't about checking off a list of houses, it's about the experience. It's about pointing out the little details—the twinkling icicle lights, the old-fashioned bulbs, or the way one house has synchronized their lights with music on the radio. Share those "oohs" and "aahs" with your passengers. Let the kids scream in delight when they spot their favorite character, or when they see a house so decked out it could probably be seen from space.

And if you don't know where to start? Easy. Most towns and cities have lists online of the best Christmas light displays. You'll often find entire areas transformed into glowing spectacles, where every house gets into the spirit. Some places even have drive-through displays where you can cruise slowly through a winter wonderland without leaving your car. But let's not forget the smaller neighborhoods either. Sometimes, the most charming displays are in the places you least expect—on the quiet, out-of-the-way streets where families are just doing it for the joy of the season, not to win any awards.

Speaking of driving, if you've got a car, pile everyone in. Pack it full of blankets, hot chocolate in thermoses, and crank up the holiday tunes. There's something about being bundled up, with the heat just barely on, sipping hot cocoa, and cruising slowly through streets filled with glowing lights that makes everything feel cozy and festive. It's a simple, old-school kind of fun that's hard to beat.

And don't think this is just a night for the kids. Even adults, who've seen it all before, can get wrapped up in the magic. Remember what it felt like as a kid to see a house decked out in lights? The awe, the wonder, the excitement? That feeling doesn't have to go away just because you've grown up. In fact, maybe it's even more special now because you understand how much work and effort goes into creating those displays. Someone took time to make their house look magical, and for that moment, you get to appreciate it.

For the ultimate Christmas light experience, don't just stick to driving around. Bundle up and go for a walk. There's something extra special about walking down a street lined with glowing houses. The cold bites at your cheeks, your breath fogs in the air, and you can get up close to all the little details you'd miss from a car. Walking also gives you the freedom to stop and take it all in without worrying about blocking traffic or missing the next turn. Plus, walking slows things down. It gives you time to savor the moment, to let the magic of the lights seep in.

If you really want to make the night special, turn it into a light-hunting game. Set challenges for everyone—find the house with the most lights, spot a display with a Santa Claus, find a house that's got a nativity scene, or count how many houses have reindeer on the roof. It adds an extra layer of fun, especially for kids, who will be eagerly scanning every display for their next "find."

And for those who want to take the experience to the next level, some cities have professionally organized light shows. These can be drive-through, walk-through, or even boat tours where entire marinas light up their vessels in holiday colors. Some places charge a small fee, but trust me, it's worth it. These are the kind of displays that make you feel like you're walking through a movie set. Lights synchronized to music, tunnels of sparkling colors, giant light-up figures of Santa, elves, and reindeer—it's all there. And the best part? Even these shows are usually pretty affordable, especially when you consider the level of production that goes into them.

Let's not forget about the free light shows either. Many parks and plazas put on dazzling displays open to the public. The trees get wrapped in glowing lights, fountains are lit up, and sometimes you even get the bonus of free holiday concerts or vendors selling hot chocolate. These community light displays offer a great excuse to get outside, get together with friends, and spend an evening soaking up the holiday atmosphere—all without spending a dime.

Another fun twist on the classic light tour is to organize a Christmas lights "crawl." Instead of just sticking to one area, map out several neighborhoods or light shows and make a night of it. Start in one spot, take your time, then move on to the next. Treat it like a bar crawl, but for Christmas lights. In between, stop somewhere for a quick bite, or bring along some homemade treats to enjoy between stops. It turns a simple drive into a full-on holiday adventure.

Now, if you want to get a little more social with your light-watching, consider organizing a Christmas lights caravan with friends or family. Everyone decorates their car with holiday lights or window clings, and you drive through the displays together. It adds an extra layer of fun, and you can all keep in touch through a group chat or walkie-talkies as you comment on the best displays, point out funny decorations, or just share in the excitement of the night. It's a simple way to make the experience feel more connected, even if you're all in separate cars.

And while you're at it, don't forget to give a little holiday cheer back to the people putting up those displays. If you see a particularly stunning house, give them a shout-out. Some people put months of effort into their decorations, and a simple "Nice lights!" goes a long way in spreading the holiday spirit. You can even leave a note or a small thank-you card in their mailbox. It's a small gesture, but it shows that their work is appreciated and helps keep the holiday cheer going strong.

Finally, here's the thing to remember about exploring Christmas light displays: it's not just about the lights themselves. It's about the shared experience. It's about bundling up with loved ones, laughing at the most over-the-top displays, or admiring the simple elegance of a single candle in a window. It's about taking a break from the holiday chaos and just enjoying something beautiful and joyful together.

You don't need to spend big bucks to have an incredible holiday experience. In fact, sometimes the best memories come from the simplest things. So grab a map, pack some snacks, cue up your favorite holiday playlist, and go explore. The lights are waiting, and the magic of the season is free for the taking.

4.3 Local Holiday Events on a Budget

The holiday season brings a whirlwind of events and festivities, each one offering a chance to connect, celebrate, and soak in the magic of the season. But let's be honest: not every holiday gathering comes with a hefty price tag. Local holiday events are often bursting with fun and excitement while remaining easy on your wallet. You can dive into a world of seasonal joy without breaking the bank. So, grab your calendar, gather your family, and get ready to experience the holidays in a budget-friendly way.

Start by tapping into the heart of your community. Towns and cities pull out all the stops when it comes to celebrating the holidays. Most of them organize festive events that are free or incredibly affordable. You might find tree-lighting ceremonies, parades, or Christmas markets right in your backyard. These gatherings are perfect for kicking off the holiday spirit. You get to mingle with neighbors, meet new friends, and celebrate the season together. So don't just sit back—get involved!

For starters, check local community boards, websites, and social media pages. These platforms are gold mines for discovering upcoming events. Local government websites often have dedicated sections for holiday activities, listing everything from small gatherings to large celebrations. You might be surprised by the number of events your area hosts. Mark your calendar for anything that catches your eye.

Let's talk about tree-lighting ceremonies. These magical events bring communities together. Crowds gather, hot cocoa flows, and excitement fills the air. You'll often see carolers singing festive tunes, children's laughter echoing around, and that moment when the lights flicker on—pure magic. It's a simple, heartwarming tradition that doesn't cost anything to enjoy. You can show up, grab a cozy spot, and soak it all in.

Don't overlook local parades either. These events often include floats, marching bands, and Santa himself making a grand entrance. Parades create a sense of community, with families lining the streets to cheer on participants. Kids get to wave at their favorite characters, and there's something truly special about the energy in the air. Many parades are free, making them an easy win for family fun. Just bundle up, grab some snacks, and enjoy the festive atmosphere.

Next up, check out local holiday markets. These pop-up markets can be fantastic for getting into the holiday spirit. Vendors set up stalls filled with handmade crafts, delicious food, and unique gifts. Even if you're not in the market to buy anything, walking through the stalls can be a delightful experience. The sights and smells alone create a festive atmosphere that can lift your spirits. Many markets also host activities like live music, craft stations for kids, or even visits with Santa. The best part? Many of these events are free to enter, so you can enjoy the festive vibes without spending much.

But let's not forget the countless smaller events happening in libraries, schools, and community centers. These places often organize holiday-themed workshops, movie nights, and even storytelling sessions. Libraries, in particular, might host book readings or craft sessions that are perfect for kids. Not only are these events low-cost, but they also provide a chance to get creative and engage with your community. Check your local library's calendar and see what holiday events are lined up. You might find a hidden gem or two.

Another great way to enjoy local holiday events on a budget is through volunteer opportunities. Many organizations host events like toy drives, soup kitchens, or community clean-ups during the holiday season. Volunteering not only gives you a chance to give back but also allows you to meet new people and create memories. Many organizations host holiday parties for their volunteers, often filled with good food and laughter. You'll feel a sense of fulfillment, and you might even walk away with new friends and connections.

If you're looking for something a little different, keep an eye out for local performances. Community theaters often put on holiday-themed shows at a fraction of the cost of big productions. You might find a charming rendition of A Christmas Carol or a holiday concert that showcases local talent. Attending these performances not only supports local artists but also offers a cozy, intimate experience that larger venues can't replicate. So, grab your loved ones, and enjoy a night filled with music and laughter without the steep ticket prices.

Don't forget to explore local parks during the holiday season. Some municipalities go all out with holiday light displays that are completely free to enjoy. Walking through a park adorned with colorful lights and festive decorations can be a memorable experience. Bring your family, pack some snacks, and stroll through the park. Capture photos of the stunning displays, let the kids run around, and bask in the glow of the season. Parks often host special events like caroling nights or outdoor movie screenings during the holidays, making them a hub for community joy.

How about hosting a potluck in conjunction with one of these events? It's a fantastic way to get everyone involved without breaking the bank. Gather friends and family and plan a potluck dinner before or after attending a local holiday event. Each person can bring a dish to share, and you'll end up with a diverse feast filled with everyone's favorite holiday recipes. It not only saves money but also creates an opportunity for everyone to share their culinary talents. Plus, sharing a meal together builds connections and adds a personal touch to your holiday celebrations.

And don't underestimate the joy of just getting out and exploring. Drive around your neighborhood or nearby areas to see how people decorate their homes for the season. It can turn into an adventure as you scout for the best displays. Challenge the family to spot the most creative decorations. You might find an inflatable Santa peeking out from behind a hedge or a lawn full of wooden reindeer. No one will complain about a little friendly competition while spreading cheer.

Another exciting idea is to participate in local charity runs or walks that often pop up during the holidays. These events usually encourage festive attire, so you can don your ugliest Christmas sweater or sparkliest holiday outfit. It's a fun way to get active, enjoy the fresh air, and contribute to a good cause at the same time. Plus, many of these events have a minimal entry fee that goes directly to charity. You'll be moving, meeting new people, and supporting your community—all while having a blast.

For those who enjoy crafts, look out for local workshops or community classes. Many craft stores or community centers offer holiday-themed crafting sessions for a small fee. Whether it's making ornaments, wreaths, or holiday cards, these workshops provide a chance to get creative and bring home something special. Even if you're not particularly crafty, participating in these events can spark your creativity and give you something unique to share with friends and family.

And let's not forget the magic of local movie nights. During the holiday season, many communities host outdoor movie screenings, showcasing classic holiday films. Bring your own blankets and snacks, and settle in for a cozy night under the stars. Even if the weather is chilly, bundling up and enjoying a film with your loved ones is a heartwarming way to spend an evening. Don't forget to check local listings for free or low-cost movie nights at parks or community centers.

Now, how about taking your holiday spirit up a notch? Consider planning a community caroling night. Gather friends, family, or neighbors and hit the streets, singing festive songs as you go. It's a simple way to spread holiday cheer, and you don't need to be a professional singer to join in on the fun. People often appreciate the gesture, and who knows? You might even inspire others to join in, creating a spontaneous holiday sing-along.

And for those who enjoy being a bit more adventurous, look for local farms or orchards that offer holiday-themed activities. Many farms host events like tree-cutting days or holiday markets. You can pick out a Christmas tree while enjoying hot cider and homemade treats. It's a fun way to create lasting memories, and you get to bring home a beautiful tree to decorate. Some farms even have petting zoos or other attractions that can make for an enjoyable day out without a hefty price tag.

Local churches or community centers often organize events as well, from candlelight services to holiday fairs. These gatherings typically welcome everyone and foster a sense of community. Even if you don't belong to a specific church, attending a service or event can provide a unique perspective on the holiday spirit. Plus, many churches host holiday concerts that showcase local talent. So, keep an eye out for their event calendars.

You can also take a look at local historical societies or museums. During the holiday season, they might host events that include historical decorations, festive tours, and even special exhibits. Some places might offer free admission days, so you can enjoy a cultural experience without spending a dime. Visiting these venues adds depth to your holiday celebrations and allows you to appreciate your community's history.

As you navigate the holiday season, remember to keep your options open. Embrace spontaneity. Sometimes the best experiences happen when you least expect them. If a friend invites you to a holiday gathering, go for it! If there's an event happening last minute that sounds fun, don't hesitate to join in. These unexpected moments often turn into cherished memories.

Finally, take the time to appreciate the spirit of giving. Many local organizations run holiday donation drives for families in need. Gather your friends and family and make it a group effort to contribute. Whether it's food, clothing, or toys, every little bit helps. Not only does this give you a chance to give back, but it also strengthens your bond with loved ones as you work together for a common cause.

So this holiday season, don't let a tight budget hold you back from enjoying all that your community has to offer. Dive into local events, participate in activities, and embrace the spirit of togetherness. Celebrate the holidays in a way that's meaningful, memorable, and budget-friendly.

Chapter 5: Spreading Holiday Cheer in Your Community

5.1 Volunteering Your Time

The holiday season isn't just about gifts and parties; it's about community and connection. When the air turns crisp and the lights start twinkling, a sense of urgency to give back fills the atmosphere. Volunteering your time during the holidays can be one of the most fulfilling experiences you can have. The best part? It doesn't cost a dime. Instead, it fills your heart with warmth, joy, and a sense of purpose.

When you volunteer, you become a part of something bigger than yourself. You connect with your neighbors and bring people together. You roll up your sleeves and dive in, making a difference in the lives of others. Start by looking for local charities, shelters, or food banks that need extra hands during the busy holiday season. These organizations often see an influx of people needing support, and they appreciate any help they can get. You'll find that these places are brimming with opportunities to lend a hand.

Want to feel the holiday spirit? Volunteer at a local soup kitchen. These kitchens serve up hot meals to those in need, especially during the colder months. Imagine bustling around, prepping food, and serving warm plates to families who might not have a holiday feast otherwise. That simple act of kindness can change someone's day. And here's the kicker: it'll change your perspective too. You'll see firsthand how your effort can impact lives, and that connection is what the holidays are all about.

Another impactful way to give back? Participate in toy drives. Many organizations host these drives to collect toys for children who might otherwise go without gifts during the holidays. You can organize a toy drive at your workplace, school, or within your neighborhood. Rally your friends and family to contribute. When you see a pile of gifts collected through your efforts, it brings a rush of excitement. Then, when the day comes to distribute the toys, you'll feel that thrill all over again as you watch smiles light up little faces.

If you're not sure where to start, check online. Websites like VolunteerMatch.org or local community boards often list opportunities to volunteer in your area. Sign up for alerts and get involved. Look for holiday events at community centers or shelters, where they might need help decorating, setting up, or even coordinating activities for families. Your hands and heart can make a world of difference.

And let's not forget the beauty of visiting nursing homes or assisted living facilities. The elderly often feel isolated during the holidays. A simple visit can uplift spirits. Organize a group of friends, sing carols, or bring along holiday treats. Share stories, listen to their experiences, and create connections. You'll discover that these interactions enrich both your lives. The joy radiating from their faces will be the best gift you receive.

If you have a knack for crafting, put those skills to work. Create handmade cards or ornaments with kids or friends and distribute them to hospitals, shelters, or nursing homes. This simple gesture can brighten someone's day. People love receiving personal touches, especially during the holidays. It's a heartfelt way to share the spirit of giving. Plus, crafting together can strengthen bonds with friends and family. It becomes an activity filled with laughter and creativity.

Some organizations host community-wide events like food drives or donation collections. Participate as a volunteer or help spread the word. Put together flyers or posts on social media to raise awareness. People often want to contribute; they just need to know how. When you rally your community to donate food, clothing, or toys, you empower others to take part in the spirit of giving. Watching the donations stack up brings an exhilarating rush of accomplishment.

Consider organizing or participating in a community clean-up. The holidays can bring a lot of waste, from packaging to decorations. Gather a group to clean up parks, streets, or community spaces. Not only does this beautify your surroundings, but it also creates a sense of camaraderie among participants. Working side by side for a common goal cultivates friendships and strengthens community ties. Plus, nothing feels better than making your neighborhood shine during the holiday season.

Don't overlook the power of simply being present. Sometimes, people just need someone to talk to or spend time with. Offer to babysit for a single parent who might need a break. Help a neighbor decorate their home or shop for groceries. Small acts of kindness go a long way, especially during this hectic time. Every little thing counts, and when you put forth the effort, you show your community that you care.

Let's talk about the animals too! Local shelters often need volunteers to help care for pets during the holiday season. If you love animals, consider donating your time at a shelter. Walk dogs, socialize cats, or help with adoption events. Animals bring joy and comfort, and spending time with them can be a refreshing break from the holiday rush. Plus, many shelters hold special events to encourage adoptions around the holidays. You might help a furry friend find their forever home!

Are you crafty or artistic? Use your talents to host a workshop or class for kids in your community. Whether it's painting, crafting, or baking, share your skills. You'll inspire creativity and build relationships with children and families. Plus, you get to spread cheer through your passions!

Another fantastic way to volunteer is to help out at holiday events or festivals. Many towns host seasonal celebrations that require extra hands. You might assist with setting up, taking tickets, or guiding guests. These events often have a festive atmosphere filled with music, food, and laughter. Getting involved gives you a front-row seat to the celebrations while allowing you to be part of something larger.

If you have specific skills or expertise, consider offering workshops or classes to teach others. If you know how to bake, offer a holiday baking class. If you're good with finances, host a budgeting workshop to help families manage holiday expenses. Sharing your knowledge with others can empower them, and you never know how much impact your guidance can have on someone's life.

Don't forget about your local schools. Reach out and see if they need help with holiday events or celebrations. Many schools organize festive gatherings or programs that require volunteers for setup or supervision. Get involved and show support for the students and educators in your community. Plus, it's a great way to connect with families in your area.

Consider coordinating a community book drive. Books can be gifts that last a lifetime. Collect gently used or new books and donate them to schools, libraries, or community centers. Organizing reading events can also inspire a love for reading among children. You might even consider setting up a cozy corner for reading sessions or storytelling events. The joy of a good story can spark imagination, especially during the holidays.

Participating in local fundraising events is another fantastic way to get involved. Many charities host holiday-themed events like walks, runs, or dinners. These gatherings not only raise funds for important causes but also build community spirit. Gather friends and family to participate together. It's a fun way to bond, while simultaneously contributing to a meaningful cause.

Don't forget about the gift of your time in small, personal ways. Offer to run errands for someone who might be struggling. Share your skills to help a neighbor with their holiday preparations. Even something as simple as offering to help wrap gifts can make someone's day a little easier.

Let's talk about mentorship too. If you have experience in a specific field or subject, consider mentoring someone in your community. It could be a high school student looking for guidance or a young adult seeking career advice. Offering your time and expertise can help others reach their goals, and you'll find the experience rewarding.

Participate in or organize community holiday parties. These gatherings foster connection among residents and can be a fun way to celebrate the season. Set up games, activities, or even potluck dinners. Invite everyone to bring a dish and share their traditions. Building relationships in your community helps create a sense of belonging, especially during the holidays.

Finally, don't underestimate the power of simply spreading kindness wherever you go. Hold the door open for someone, smile at strangers, or share compliments. These small gestures can create a ripple effect, spreading joy and warmth throughout your community. When you focus on giving, you inspire others to do the same.

So, as you navigate this holiday season, remember the importance of giving back. Volunteering your time can transform lives, including your own. You'll create connections, foster community spirit, and fill your heart with joy. Dive in, find opportunities to help, and let the magic of the season shine through your actions. Your efforts will not only bring cheer to others but also create lasting memories for yourself.

5.2 Making Handmade Cards for Neighbors

Nothing screams holiday spirit like a colorful card slipped into a mailbox or handed to a neighbor with a smile. When you think about spreading joy, making handmade cards is one of the simplest yet most heartfelt ways to do it. You don't need a fancy printing press or graphic design skills. Just some creativity, a few basic supplies, and a willingness to share your warmth and goodwill. That's it. Let's dive into how you can bring cheer to your neighbors, one handmade card at a time.

First, gather your materials. You don't need to break the bank for this project. Grab some cardstock or any sturdy paper you have lying around. Old birthday cards, leftover wrapping paper, or even plain printer paper work great. You can cut them down to size for cards. The beauty of handmade cards is that they come from you, imperfections and all. Don't sweat the small stuff. Look for scissors, glue, markers, and any other fun embellishments you might have. Ribbons, stickers, or glitter can add flair. Let your imagination run wild!

Set up your workspace. Find a cozy spot in your home where you feel inspired. Lay out all your materials, and don't forget to crank up some festive music. The right tunes can really get your creative juices flowing. Light some candles or hang up twinkling lights if you want to create that holiday vibe. Comfort is key!

Now, think about what you want to express in your cards. Simple messages go a long way. You might write "Happy Holidays," "Season's Greetings," or "Wishing You Joy and Peace." Keep it personal. Consider adding a short note expressing your appreciation for your neighbors or a memory you share. People love feeling valued and remembered. Your words can brighten someone's day more than you realize.

If you have kids, involve them in the process. This becomes a family bonding experience while teaching the importance of giving back. Set up a mini card-making station. Kids can draw, color, and create to their hearts' content. Encourage them to be silly, draw funny pictures, or write little messages. The joy of creating together can turn into cherished memories. Plus, kids often have a unique way of expressing love and joy, so their contributions will undoubtedly add something special to the cards.

Once you've created your cards, it's time to get creative with the envelopes. If you don't have envelopes, no problem. You can make simple envelopes by folding paper into a pocket shape. Just seal it with tape or a sticker. If you do have envelopes, consider decorating them with doodles or stamps. Personalizing the envelope adds an extra touch, showing that you put thought into it before even opening the card.

Now, you're ready to deliver! The excitement builds as you think about your neighbors opening their mailboxes and discovering your handmade treasures. Grab a friend or family member to join you for this part. It's more fun to deliver cards together. Plus, you can share laughs and stories along the way.

Start with those closest to you. Knock on doors and hand the cards directly to your neighbors. If they're home, a quick chat can brighten the moment. Ask them how they're celebrating the holidays this year, or share a lighthearted memory. This face-to-face interaction strengthens community bonds and creates a sense of belonging.

If you encounter neighbors you don't know well, that's okay! A simple smile and a warm "Happy Holidays!" while handing them the card is perfect. Sometimes, this small gesture can break the ice and lead to deeper connections later. You'll be surprised at how grateful they are for your thoughtfulness.

What about those neighbors who might not be around? Maybe they're traveling or busy with family. Just slip your card into their mailbox or leave it on their doorstep. The element of surprise makes it all the more delightful! When they return, they'll find your card waiting for them, a little piece of holiday cheer.

Don't forget about the elderly neighbors or those who might be isolated during the holidays. A handwritten card can mean the world to someone who might not have many visitors. If you know their address but don't feel comfortable knocking, mail the card. It's a small effort that can brighten their day.

Consider hosting a card-making party! Invite friends, family, or neighbors over for a fun afternoon of crafting. Lay out all your supplies and let everyone get creative. Serve some holiday snacks and drinks to keep the festive mood alive. Sharing ideas and laughter while making cards adds an extra layer of joy to the experience.

Encourage guests to create cards for specific causes as well. Organizations like local hospitals or shelters often appreciate donations of handmade cards, especially during the holidays. You can also create cards for veterans or those in assisted living facilities. Spread the cheer beyond just your immediate community.

If you want to take it a step further, gather your friends for a neighborhood card drive. Set a goal for how many cards you want to make and distribute. This kind of collaboration amplifies your impact. You'll not only spread cheer to your neighbors but also strengthen connections with your friends and family.

Once you've made your cards and distributed them, take a moment to reflect. Think about how you felt creating them and sharing that joy with others. The act of making something with your hands fosters a connection to the people receiving it. You've taken time out of your day to create something special. That effort, no matter how small, goes a long way.

Share your experience on social media. Post pictures of your card-making process or your finished cards. Use hashtags like HandmadeHolidayCards or SpreadCheer. Encourage others to join in, creating a ripple effect of creativity and kindness throughout your community. You might inspire someone else to pick up some supplies and get crafting, leading to even more joy.

What happens next? You'll notice that as you spread joy, it often comes back to you. Your neighbors will appreciate the gesture, and you might find that they respond with their own cards or small acts of kindness. That's the beauty of community—when you give, you often receive in unexpected ways.

This holiday season, let's make it all about connection. Your handmade cards can act as bridges between you and your neighbors. You never know what struggles they might be facing or how much a simple card can uplift their spirits. The world can feel isolated, especially during the busy holiday season. Your effort to reach out breaks down those walls, creating a sense of belonging and camaraderie.

You don't need to be a professional artist or a poet to make an impact. Your authentic effort and genuine care shine through. Even the simplest drawings or messages can evoke powerful emotions. So grab your supplies and start creating. The holiday season is the perfect time to share your creativity and kindness with those around you.

As the holidays approach, remember that it's the little things that matter. Making handmade cards for your neighbors doesn't require a grand gesture. Instead, it's about the thought and love you put into each creation. So, roll up your sleeves, unleash your inner artist, and spread joy through your cards. You'll find that each card you make strengthens your community and fills your heart with holiday cheer.

5.3 Random Acts of Kindness

As the holiday season approaches, a wave of generosity sweeps through communities. People feel a desire to give back, to spread joy, and to connect with one another. Among all the glitter and glamour of the holidays, random acts of kindness shine the brightest. These small gestures, often unexpected, have the power to transform not just the recipient's day but also your own. Imagine brightening someone's day with a simple act, a genuine smile, or an offer of help. That's what this time of year is all about.

Let's get into the spirit of giving. Start with something as simple as paying for the coffee of the person behind you in line. It's a tiny act, yet the ripple effect it creates can be immense. Picture the surprise on their face when they learn that someone just brightened their morning. That single act can inspire them to pay it forward, continuing the cycle of kindness. It's contagious!

Another great idea? Leave a positive note on a neighbor's doorstep or in a community space. A little encouragement goes a long way. It could be a quote that resonates or a reminder that someone cares. You might even write "You're doing amazing!" or "Have a great day!" Make it colorful and cheerful. You'll brighten someone's day without even being there to witness it.

How about organizing a community clean-up day? Grab some friends, neighbors, or family members and tackle a local park or street that needs a little TLC. Bring trash bags, gloves, and your favorite tunes. Not only will you beautify your community, but you'll also enjoy some quality time with loved ones. As you work together, you'll create connections and memories that will last long after the holidays have passed.

Don't overlook the impact of donating your time. Reach out to local charities or organizations and offer to help with their holiday events. Whether it's wrapping gifts for children in need, serving meals at a soup kitchen, or organizing donations for families, your hands can make a world of difference. The gratitude you'll receive in return will warm your heart. Plus, you'll likely meet others who share your passion for helping, which can lead to lasting friendships.

Here's a fun twist: set up a surprise potluck at work or with friends. Gather everyone together and encourage them to bring a dish to share. It fosters a sense of community and gives everyone a chance to showcase their cooking skills. The best part? Sharing food brings people together. You'll enjoy laughter, conversation, and maybe even some new recipes along the way.

What about offering to help a neighbor? Maybe they're struggling to carry groceries or could use a hand with home repairs. Jump in and lend a hand. It doesn't take much time or effort to make a significant impact. The simple act of being there for someone can ease their burdens, making the holidays a little brighter. You'll create a bond that lasts long after the season ends.

Ever thought about leaving some spare change or a small gift card at a drive-thru? Imagine the joy of a stranger finding that surprise! A few bucks might not seem like much to you, but it could make someone's day. It's a way of saying, "Hey, I see you. I care." Random acts like this, though simple, ripple out to affect more than just one person.

Take it a step further and get the kids involved. Host a "kindness day" where everyone chooses an act of kindness to complete. It could be as simple as complimenting a stranger or baking cookies for someone in the neighborhood. When children see their parents or guardians performing kind acts, they internalize those behaviors and carry them into adulthood. You'll nurture a generation of compassionate individuals ready to spread joy.

Got a few extra blankets or jackets? Donate them to a local shelter. As temperatures drop, many people find themselves in need of warm clothing. By sharing what you have, you help others stay warm and comfortable. This simple gesture can provide relief during an otherwise challenging time. Plus, it feels good to know you're making a difference.

Think about organizing a holiday gift drive. Rally your friends, family, and coworkers to donate toys, clothing, or food items for families in need. Set a goal, create a collection box, and watch as the community comes together to support each other. Deliver the collected items to local charities or organizations, and witness firsthand the gratitude and joy that comes with your efforts. It's a rewarding experience, and you'll build connections with those around you.

If you're tech-savvy, use social media to spread kindness. Start a local "kindness challenge." Encourage others to share their acts of kindness online, using a specific hashtag. The visibility encourages participation and creates a community of givers. Share your experiences and inspire others to follow suit. When you highlight kindness, it motivates people to act.

Next time you visit a store, consider leaving a kind note for the employees. Thank them for their hard work, especially during the busy holiday season. A small gesture can boost morale and remind them that their efforts matter. Handwritten notes convey warmth and appreciation that will brighten their day.

Think about bringing some joy to the four-legged friends in your community. Collect donations of pet food or supplies for local animal shelters. You can also volunteer to walk dogs or play with the animals waiting for their forever homes. Spending time with them not only enriches their lives but also brings you immense joy. Animals have a unique way of connecting us to our humanity.

As you navigate the holiday season, take a moment to reflect on those who may feel lonely or isolated. Consider reaching out to elderly neighbors or friends who might not have family nearby. A simple phone call or visit can mean the world. Bring them cookies, watch a movie together, or just sit and chat. Your presence can provide companionship and comfort during a time when many feel alone.

Engage in secret giving! Leave small treats or gifts on doorsteps, with no one knowing where they came from. It adds an element of surprise and excitement to the season. The recipient will marvel at the thoughtfulness of a mystery giver, and you'll feel a sense of satisfaction knowing you made someone smile without seeking recognition.

If you're crafty, why not create handmade items to give away? Whether it's knitting scarves, making candles, or crafting ornaments, your handiwork will carry your personal touch. This effort shows that you invested your time and energy, making the gift extra special. It doesn't have to be perfect; what matters is the thought behind it.

Here's another idea: host a community game night or movie marathon. Invite neighbors to gather for some fun and laughter. Bring snacks, and encourage everyone to bring their favorite games or films. It's a great way to build camaraderie and create memories together. Plus, the laughter shared during these activities strengthens community ties.

Feeling adventurous? Write messages of kindness on sticky notes and place them in random locations throughout your community. Whether it's on a bathroom mirror, a park bench, or a library book, these little notes can brighten someone's day. They're like mini surprises waiting to be discovered, providing inspiration and encouragement to anyone who comes across them.

When you're out shopping, hold the door for someone carrying a heavy load. Lend a hand, help carry packages, or offer your cart to someone who needs it. Simple gestures create connections between strangers. It reminds us that we're all in this together, especially during the hectic holiday season.

Another simple act is to provide meals for those who are struggling. If you know a family that could use a warm meal, offer to cook a dinner for them. Drop it off with a smile and a kind word. Food nourishes not only the body but also the spirit. A hearty meal can bring comfort and warmth during challenging times.

Consider volunteering to help a local nonprofit organization with their holiday events. They might need assistance wrapping gifts, setting up events, or organizing donations. You'll make valuable contributions while learning more about the organizations in your community. Plus, you'll meet like-minded people who share your passion for helping others.

Engage in community gardening if you have access to outdoor space. Gather neighbors to beautify a local park or garden. Plant flowers, herbs, or vegetables that everyone can enjoy. This collaborative effort fosters teamwork, and the outcome is a beautiful space for the community to enjoy. Gardening together strengthens bonds while creating something wonderful.

Let's not forget the power of sharing stories. Reach out to someone in your community, an elderly neighbor, or even a stranger. Ask them about their favorite holiday memories. Listen closely as they share their experiences. It shows that you value their stories and helps forge connections. Sometimes, people just need someone to listen, and your interest can brighten their day.

Remember, kindness is not limited to grand gestures. Small, everyday actions add up to create a wave of goodwill. Hold onto that mindset as you approach the holiday season. The magic lies in the little things. A smile, a compliment, or a helping hand can mean the world to someone in need.

If you're looking to create lasting change in your community, consider establishing a "kindness committee" with friends or neighbors. This group can brainstorm new ideas for spreading kindness year-round. Regularly organizing acts of kindness can foster a culture of giving in your community, transforming how you all interact with each other.

After the holidays, don't let the spirit of kindness fade away. Continue to look for ways to incorporate random acts of kindness into your daily life. Small actions can lead to big changes over time. Consistently choosing kindness fosters a positive environment and encourages others to follow suit.

As you embrace the holiday season, remember the power of your actions. Random acts of kindness create waves of positivity, spreading joy not just to individuals but throughout the community. You might never know

Chapter 6: Savoring the Simple Joys of Christmas

6.1 Creating a Cozy Holiday Atmosphere

The holiday season rolls around each year, and with it comes the chance to create a warm and inviting atmosphere that transforms your home into a festive haven. Picture this: twinkling lights, the aroma of freshly baked cookies wafting through the air, and the sounds of laughter and holiday music filling the rooms. Creating a cozy holiday atmosphere isn't about spending a fortune. It's about tapping into your creativity, utilizing what you have, and spreading warmth and joy. Let's explore how to turn your space into a sanctuary of holiday cheer.

Start with the basics: lighting. There's something magical about soft, warm lighting that sets the tone for the entire season. Ditch the harsh overhead lights and opt for string lights, candles, or even lanterns. Wrap string lights around banisters, drape them over mantels, or hang them in windows. It's as if stars have come down to join your festivities! If you're feeling adventurous, use a few jars to create DIY lanterns. Fill them with fairy lights or place a candle inside. The flickering glow adds an intimate touch, making any space feel special.

Next, let's talk about scents. The right aromas can evoke memories and feelings of nostalgia. Bake cookies or make a batch of hot cocoa to fill your home with those comforting smells. If baking isn't your thing, simmer a pot of water with cinnamon sticks, cloves, and orange peels on the stove. The aroma will wrap around you like a warm hug. For an extra touch, consider using essential oils. A few drops of pine or peppermint in a diffuser can create an uplifting and festive ambiance.

Now, let's add some festive decorations. You don't have to go overboard to make your space feel cheerful. Grab a few holiday decorations you already own and display them creatively. Arrange them on shelves, tabletops, or mantels. Think about using natural elements too. Fresh pine branches or holly can bring a touch of the outdoors inside. Place them in vases or simply lay them across your table as a centerpiece. Incorporate items that resonate with your holiday traditions, be it ornaments, figurines, or garlands. Each piece adds a personal touch that tells your story.

Creating a cozy atmosphere isn't just about visual elements; it's also about comfort. Stock up on cozy blankets and pillows. Drape them over your couch or chairs, inviting everyone to snuggle up. Think about textures—soft, fluffy, and inviting. Choose colors that remind you of the season, like deep reds, greens, or sparkling golds. When you create a space that feels comfortable, people want to linger and enjoy each other's company.

Let's not forget about music. The right tunes can elevate the atmosphere in an instant. Curate a playlist of your favorite holiday songs, mixing classic carols with contemporary hits. Play it softly in the background while you cook, decorate, or simply relax with family. Music brings everyone together, encouraging singing, dancing, and all-around joy. It's a simple way to make the house feel alive.

Consider adding personal touches that evoke memories. Display family photos from past holidays or hang ornaments that hold special significance. Maybe you have a handmade ornament from your child or a trinket from a memorable trip. These elements invite conversation and nostalgia, allowing everyone to share stories and reminisce about the past. It's about creating a space where everyone feels connected and valued.

Gather your loved ones for a crafting session to create homemade decorations. It can be a fun and engaging activity, especially with kids. Use items from nature—pinecones, branches, or leaves—to make festive decorations. Create garlands, wreaths, or even simple ornaments. This not only brings creativity into your home but also allows for quality time spent together. As you craft, share stories and laughter, and watch as your space fills with love and joy.

On the food front, embrace the joy of cooking together. Gather family members in the kitchen and whip up your favorite holiday treats. Whether it's baking cookies, making gingerbread houses, or preparing a festive meal, the kitchen becomes the heart of the home. The act of cooking together fosters connection. Share recipes, traditions, and laughter while creating delicious memories.

Consider hosting a cozy movie night. Choose holiday classics that everyone loves. Set up a comfortable viewing area with plenty of blankets and cushions. Prepare popcorn, hot cocoa, or other festive snacks. As you gather to watch the movies, enjoy the shared experience and the warmth of togetherness. It's these moments that create lasting memories and strengthen family bonds.

When it comes to gift-giving, keep it simple and meaningful. Rather than splurging on expensive gifts, focus on thoughtful gestures. Handwritten letters expressing gratitude, small homemade treats, or simple crafts can have a profound impact. It's not about the price tag; it's about the thought and love behind the gift. The recipients will appreciate the effort, and it enhances the cozy atmosphere you're creating.

Incorporate a gratitude element into your holiday celebration. Create a gratitude tree where everyone can hang notes expressing what they're thankful for. Use colorful paper and string to display these notes prominently in your living space. This practice encourages reflection and appreciation, reminding everyone of the blessings they share. As you read through the notes together, you'll create an even deeper sense of connection and joy.

If you have the space, set up a cozy reading nook. Fill it with blankets, pillows, and your favorite holiday books. Encourage family members to spend time there, reading aloud or curling up with a good book. This tranquil space invites relaxation and fosters a love for stories, allowing everyone to escape into a world of imagination.

As the holidays approach, take a moment to reflect on your traditions. What do you cherish the most? Are there activities that hold a special place in your heart? Perhaps it's caroling, attending a local holiday market, or visiting a nearby tree farm. Embrace these traditions and incorporate them into your holiday routine. They help create continuity and a sense of belonging that enhances the cozy atmosphere you're cultivating.

Creating a cozy holiday atmosphere is about prioritizing connection over perfection. Let go of the need to create a picture-perfect setting. Embrace the messiness of life, and focus on what truly matters—time spent with loved ones. This is what the holidays are about. The laughter, the stories, and the shared experiences will be what everyone remembers, not how perfectly arranged your decorations were.

Bring the joy of baking into your holiday traditions. Host a cookie exchange with friends or neighbors. Each person brings a batch of their favorite cookies, and you swap them. It's a fantastic way to try new flavors while enjoying each other's company. As you sample and share, the atmosphere becomes filled with laughter and the sweet aroma of freshly baked goods.

Take some time to indulge in self-care during this bustling season. Create a cozy retreat for yourself, even if it's just for an hour. Light some candles, wrap yourself in a soft blanket, and enjoy a cup of tea. Whether you choose to read, meditate, or simply sit in silence, this moment of calm is essential. It reminds you to savor the season and embrace the simple joys of life.

As the holidays unfold, consider hosting a "neighbors' night in." Invite those living nearby to join you for an evening of fun. Share food, play games, and create a sense of community. It's an opportunity to connect with those around you, building relationships that go beyond the holiday season. Everyone will leave feeling uplifted, knowing they belong to a caring community.

As you savor the simple joys of Christmas, remember to capture the moments. Take photos, write in a holiday journal, or create a scrapbook. Documenting your experiences allows you to relive the magic long after the decorations come down. It's a reminder of the love and joy shared during this special time.

Keep an open heart. Embrace the spontaneous moments that arise during the holidays. Whether it's a last-minute gathering, a surprise visit from friends, or an impromptu snowball fight, these unplanned events often become the most cherished memories. Allow yourself to be present and enjoy the journey.

As the season comes to a close, take the lessons learned from creating a cozy atmosphere with you. The warmth, connection, and love shared during this time can continue throughout the year. It's all about fostering relationships and cherishing the simple joys in life. Carry that spirit with you, and let it guide your actions as you move into the new year.

Creating a cozy holiday atmosphere doesn't require extravagant spending or elaborate plans. It's about the intention behind your actions, the love you share, and the connections you nurture. Embrace the simple joys, focus on what truly matters, and watch as your home becomes a sanctuary of warmth and happiness. With every decoration hung, every meal shared, and every moment spent with loved ones, you'll craft a holiday season that feels magical.

So, this holiday season, prioritize coziness. Revel in the simplicity of togetherness and connection. Whether through lighting, scents, decorations, or cherished traditions, create an environment that fosters love and joy. Savor the little things, embrace spontaneity, and make memories that last a lifetime. This is what Christmas is all about. Enjoy every moment, and let the cozy spirit fill your heart.

6.2 Enjoying Homemade Holiday Treats

The smell of fresh cookies wafting through the house. The laughter of family gathered in the kitchen. The joyful chaos that comes from mixing ingredients and sharing stories. This is what makes the holiday season feel special. Homemade treats bring a unique warmth to your home. They provide a way to connect, to share, and to celebrate. So, let's roll up our sleeves and get baking!

The process starts with choosing the right recipes. Forget the fancy magazines and elaborate cookbooks. Instead, think about your favorite holiday treats from childhood. What cookies made your mouth water? What desserts do you associate with family gatherings? Whether it's classic gingerbread cookies, rich chocolate fudge, or a simple batch of sugar cookies, these familiar recipes create a comforting backdrop for your celebrations.

Gather your loved ones. Make it a family affair. Everyone can contribute. Assign roles: one person can measure ingredients, another can mix, and someone else can decorate. When everyone pitches in, the kitchen buzzes with energy. It's not just about baking; it's about sharing laughter and creating memories. Plus, you'll have a chance to teach the younger generation the recipes that hold meaning for you. Pass down the family secrets while making new ones.

You don't need to stick to traditional recipes either. Get creative! Use what you have in the pantry. Do you have leftover candy from Halloween? Chop it up and add it to your cookie dough. Got a stash of dried fruit? Toss it in the mix. Experimenting in the kitchen brings a sense of adventure. Each batch becomes a unique creation, and who knows—you might just stumble upon a new family favorite.

Let's not forget about presentation. Homemade treats don't have to be perfect to look beautiful. Use your imagination to package them nicely. Find colorful containers or decorative tins and fill them with your baked goods. Tie them up with ribbons, or add handwritten labels to give them a personal touch. When you share these goodies, you're not just giving treats; you're sharing a piece of your heart.

Consider hosting a holiday baking party. Invite friends, family, or neighbors over to create a festive atmosphere. Set up baking stations with different recipes, and let everyone rotate. It's a great way to bond and learn from each other's culinary skills. While the treats bake, enjoy hot cocoa or mulled wine, and let the holiday spirit flow. The laughter and chatter will fill your home, turning it into a hub of warmth and joy.

When the treats are ready, gather everyone for a taste test. Create a cozy setting with warm drinks and comfy blankets. Set up a table adorned with your baked goods, and invite everyone to dig in. As you sample each creation, share stories about the memories tied to those recipes. This moment of togetherness transforms simple baked goods into cherished experiences.

Don't limit your homemade treats to just cookies or desserts. Think beyond the traditional. Homemade granola or spiced nuts make excellent gifts. Package them up nicely and give them to neighbors or friends. When you hand over these treats, you're sharing your time and effort, and that adds a special layer of meaning.

If you're feeling adventurous, try making holiday-themed treats that are unique to your traditions. Perhaps a batch of rugelach, a yule log, or a savory holiday bread. Embrace the flavors that resonate with your heritage. Not only do these treats satisfy your cravings, but they also keep cultural traditions alive. Sharing these dishes can spark conversations about family history, creating deeper connections with those around you.

Let's talk about the joy of decorating holiday treats. Grab some frosting, sprinkles, and edible glitter. Let everyone get creative with their designs. Kids love to unleash their imaginations, and adults can get in on the fun too. Make it a friendly competition: who can create the most outrageous cookie? The silliness and laughter will echo in the kitchen, leaving everyone feeling uplifted and connected.

Once you've decorated your cookies, consider hosting a cookie exchange. Invite friends and family to bring their homemade treats to share. Set a date, and make it a festive gathering. Everyone leaves with a variety of goodies, and you get to enjoy the creativity of others. This shared experience fosters community and brings a taste of different flavors to your table.

Remember that baking isn't just about the end result. It's about the entire process—the joy of mixing, the anticipation while waiting for cookies to bake, and the satisfaction of enjoying something made with love. Even if a batch doesn't turn out as planned, the experience is still valuable. Share a laugh over the "flop," and appreciate the memories created during the process.

The holiday season often brings a whirlwind of activities, and sometimes it's easy to forget to slow down. Baking homemade treats is a perfect excuse to pause, breathe, and savor the moment. As the aroma fills your kitchen, take a moment to reflect. Enjoy the little things—watch the snow fall outside, listen to holiday music in the background, or simply share stories with those around you.

When you find the time to enjoy your treats, don't rush through it. Savor each bite. Let the flavors linger on your palate. Whether it's a gooey chocolate chip cookie or a spiced pumpkin pie, take a moment to appreciate the effort that went into making it. Share those moments with others. Compliment someone's baking skills, or reminisce about the family traditions tied to the flavors you're enjoying.

After the holiday festivities are over, don't let those homemade treats go to waste. Organize a gathering where you can share leftovers. Invite friends and neighbors to partake in a "dessert potluck." It's an opportunity to reconnect and enjoy each other's company while indulging in all those delicious goodies.

As you savor those simple joys of Christmas, consider giving back. Use your baking skills to help those in need. Prepare a batch of treats to donate to a local charity, shelter, or food bank. The act of giving enriches the holiday spirit and connects you to your community in meaningful ways. Plus, it allows you to share the joy of your homemade goodies with those who might appreciate them most.

Don't forget to take care of yourself during this busy time. Indulge in the treats you bake, but also balance it out with some nutritious options. Consider making a batch of healthy snacks—like energy balls or homemade granola bars—to enjoy amidst all the sweets. Find joy in nourishing your body while celebrating the season.

The holiday season offers a chance to create traditions centered around food and love. If you have kids, involve them in the process from start to finish. Let them pick recipes, decorate cookies, or help with cleanup. These shared experiences create lasting memories. Watching their excitement as they mix ingredients or decorate treats is heartwarming.

In the rush of the holiday season, try to carve out time for a "treat day." Choose a day to dedicate to baking and indulging in homemade goodies. Gather your family or friends, and make a day of it. As you roll dough and sprinkle flour everywhere, let the laughter fill your home. Create a playlist of your favorite holiday tunes and let the music guide you through the day.

Consider creating a holiday recipe book. Document your favorite holiday treats, along with stories and memories tied to each recipe.

Over the years, this book can become a cherished family heirloom. It preserves the traditions you create and serves as a reminder of the love and joy shared through cooking. Each page will tell a story, inviting future generations to join in the celebration of homemade goodness.

As the holiday season comes to a close, take a moment to reflect on the joy of homemade treats. Appreciate the laughter, love, and creativity that filled your kitchen. Embrace the moments spent with family and friends as you crafted delicious memories together. The simple act of baking has the power to create connections that last a lifetime.

Enjoying homemade holiday treats isn't just about satisfying your sweet tooth; it's about the love, care, and effort you put into every bite. Whether you're sharing them with loved ones or giving back to the community, each treat becomes a symbol of connection and celebration. As you continue to savor the simple joys of Christmas, remember that it's the moments shared over homemade goodies that make the season truly special.

So this holiday season, get in the kitchen. Bake those cookies, create those treats, and relish in the warmth of homemade goodness. Embrace the messiness, the laughter, and the connections. Create traditions that resonate with you, and share them with those you love. Every bite becomes a piece of joy—a reminder of the simple pleasures that make Christmas magical.

6.3 Reflecting on the Spirit of Christmas

———————

Christmas rolls around, and everything feels alive. Twinkling lights blanket houses, while the scent of pine needles fills the air. It's a time when hearts swell with joy, and the spirit of giving weaves through our everyday lives. But amidst the frenzy of shopping, parties, and meal planning, it's easy to lose sight of what the season truly represents. Taking a moment to reflect on the spirit of Christmas can help you find depth in this bustling time.

The holiday season opens up a space for gratitude. Look around you. What do you see? Family gathered around the table, friends sharing laughter, and community members reaching out to one another. It's a beautiful reminder of the connections we often take for granted. Focus on the little moments: the warmth of a hug, the joy in a shared story, and the comfort found in familiar traditions. These instances don't cost a dime, yet they hold immeasurable value.

Take time to sit in silence. Pause your holiday rush and find a cozy spot. Whether it's with a warm cup of cocoa in hand or wrapped in a soft blanket, embrace the stillness. Reflect on your experiences over the past year. What challenges did you face? What victories did you celebrate? Allow yourself to feel both the highs and the lows. This reflection gives context to your current joy and brings a deeper understanding of the season.

What does Christmas mean to you? Think back to your childhood memories—the excitement of unwrapping gifts, the joy of singing carols, or the warmth of family gatherings. Those feelings still exist, waiting to be rekindled. Dive into those memories, and let them wash over you like a gentle wave. They shape your perspective on the holiday and connect you to the essence of the season.

While you bask in nostalgia, consider the traditions that have been passed down through generations. Have you carried any of them forward? Perhaps your grandmother made a particular dish every Christmas Eve, or your family volunteered at a local charity every December. Embrace those customs and add your twist. Maybe you start a new tradition that reflects who you are today. Let your experiences shape the season in a way that resonates with you.

The spirit of Christmas also brings a sense of community. Reach out to your neighbors or friends, especially those who might feel isolated during this time. A simple phone call or a heartfelt note can go a long way. Offer to help someone who may struggle during the holidays. Whether it's lending a hand to decorate, share a meal, or just sit and chat, your kindness amplifies the holiday spirit.

This is the season to give back. Reflect on how you can make a positive impact on others. Volunteer at a local shelter, participate in a food drive, or donate to a charity. When you step outside your own bubble, you'll discover a sense of fulfillment that comes from helping others. Nothing compares to the warmth that fills your heart when you make someone else's holiday a little brighter.

In the spirit of giving, consider creating thoughtful gifts that reflect your love and appreciation for those around you. Homemade treats, handwritten letters, or a simple photo album filled with memories showcase how much you value your relationships. These gifts don't need to be extravagant; they just need to come from the heart. The joy you find in giving is contagious and creates a ripple effect in your community.

Don't overlook the beauty of simple pleasures during this season. Stroll through your neighborhood to admire the decorations. Listen to carolers singing classic tunes. Spend a quiet evening gazing at the stars with a loved one. These moments often slip by in the holiday rush, but they hold profound significance. They remind you of the beauty that exists in the world and encourage you to cherish every fleeting moment.

The act of reflection can guide you in setting intentions for the new year. As Christmas lights twinkle in the distance, think about the goals and aspirations you want to achieve. What lessons did you learn this year? What do you want to carry forward? Jot down your thoughts and create a vision for the future. The spirit of Christmas infuses your dreams with hope, encouraging you to pursue your passions with vigor.

As you gather with family and friends, share your reflections. Open up conversations about what Christmas means to each person. You might uncover stories that inspire you, teach you, or connect you in unexpected ways. Each person carries a unique perspective that enriches the holiday experience. This exchange creates a deeper sense of understanding and strengthens your bonds with those you love.

While the lights flicker and laughter fills the air, remember that Christmas also has its challenges. It's easy to get swept away by the pressure of expectations, both from yourself and others. Acknowledge those feelings without judgment. Accept that it's okay to feel overwhelmed or stressed during the holidays. Reach out to others who might feel the same way. Sharing your experiences can lighten the burden and foster a sense of camaraderie.

Consider how you can cultivate mindfulness during this hectic season. Slow down and savor each experience. When you bake cookies, focus on the feel of the dough, the aroma of cinnamon, and the laughter echoing around you. When you wrap gifts, enjoy the texture of the paper, the satisfaction of a perfectly tied bow, and the anticipation of watching someone open it. The more you engage with the present moment, the more joy you'll find in even the simplest tasks.

Music has a unique ability to lift spirits. Create a holiday playlist filled with your favorite tunes—classic carols, contemporary songs, or even instrumental pieces that bring you peace. Play it in the background while you decorate, cook, or spend time with loved ones. Let the music fill your space with warmth and happiness, reminding you of the joy that the season brings.

As you reflect on the spirit of Christmas, consider your own personal growth. How have you evolved over the years? What lessons have you learned that you can carry into the next year? Embrace your journey, acknowledging both your successes and struggles. This reflection allows you to celebrate who you are and provides clarity on who you want to become.

Incorporate acts of kindness into your daily routine during the holiday season. Hold the door open for someone, smile at a stranger, or offer a compliment. These small gestures may seem insignificant, but they can brighten someone's day. As you spread kindness, you'll find that the holiday spirit grows within you. Each positive interaction contributes to a collective atmosphere of love and support.

Take a moment to connect with nature. Go for a walk in a nearby park, breathe in the crisp winter air, and appreciate the beauty of the season. Nature offers a peaceful backdrop for reflection and serves as a reminder of the cycles of life. Just as the earth takes a rest in winter, you too can find rejuvenation through introspection.

As the year draws to a close, set aside time to express gratitude. Write down the things you're thankful for—big and small. Reflect on the people who have impacted your life, the experiences that have shaped you, and the lessons learned along the way. Gratitude has a profound way of shifting your perspective, helping you to focus on abundance rather than lack.

Engage in meaningful conversations with loved ones. Ask about their favorite Christmas memories, their hopes for the future, and their thoughts on the year ahead. Sharing these intimate moments strengthens connections and deepens your understanding of one another. Every shared story weaves a richer tapestry of relationships, reminding you that you're never alone.

As Christmas approaches, remind yourself that it's not about the material gifts you receive but the love you give and share. The spirit of Christmas thrives in kindness, compassion, and connection. When you shift your focus from what's on your wish list to how you can uplift those around you, you'll experience a transformation. The essence of the holiday season will fill your heart with joy and fulfillment.

Throughout the chaos of the holidays, remember to prioritize self-care. Your well-being matters, and it's essential to recharge during busy times. Schedule moments just for yourself. Whether it's curling up with a good book, practicing yoga, or meditating, taking time for yourself helps you show up more fully for others.

Think about the legacy you want to leave behind. How do you want to be remembered? The spirit of Christmas encourages you to cultivate a legacy of love, kindness, and compassion. Live each day in a way that reflects those values. By embodying the spirit of giving, you inspire others to do the same, creating a ripple effect that extends far beyond the holiday season.

As you prepare to welcome a new year, don't forget to celebrate your journey. Acknowledge your achievements, both big and small. Reflect on how far you've come and the challenges you've overcome. Every experience contributes to your growth, and recognizing that progress fosters a sense of empowerment.

Christmas offers a unique opportunity to reflect on the spirit of giving and the connections that bind us together. As you gather with loved ones, engage in thoughtful discussions, and express gratitude, you'll uncover the true meaning of the season. Remember to savor the simple joys—the laughter, the warmth, and the love.

In the end, the spirit of Christmas lives on in your heart. Carry that joy into the new year, and let it guide you in your relationships, your actions, and your dreams. When you reflect on the season with intention, you'll find that its lessons extend far beyond the holiday itself. Embrace the spirit of Christmas all year long, and allow it to shape your life in beautiful ways.

Conclusion

In closing this book, let's take a moment to reflect on everything we've explored together. The holiday season, especially Christmas, carries a unique magic. It has a way of uniting us, weaving together our diverse experiences, traditions, and joys. We've talked about ways to embrace the spirit of giving while keeping our wallets happy.

Christmas shouldn't feel like a race against the clock or a competition for who can outdo the other. It's about connection, laughter, and love. Each chapter reminds us that we can celebrate without breaking the bank. We can find joy in the simple things. A cozy gathering with friends, a potluck dinner, or a game night creates memories that last a lifetime. These moments matter. They enrich our lives in ways that expensive gifts can never match.

As we reflect on our community, it's clear that the spirit of Christmas goes beyond our immediate circle. Volunteering and reaching out to neighbors bring us closer together. A simple act of kindness can ripple through our neighborhoods, touching lives in unexpected ways. When we extend our hands and hearts, we create an environment where everyone feels valued and included. The joy of giving doesn't always come from a monetary exchange. Sometimes, it's a listening ear, a warm meal, or a handwritten card that means the world to someone.

Throughout the pages of this book, we've seen that the holiday season is a chance to celebrate who we are and where we come from. Our traditions shape us, and sharing them with others fosters understanding and appreciation. It's about bridging gaps and breaking down barriers.

When we embrace our roots and honor our heritage, we invite others to join in.

This season encourages us to look inward, reflect on what matters, and redefine what success looks like. It's not about the biggest tree or the most elaborate decorations. Instead, it's about how we feel in our homes, surrounded by loved ones, laughter echoing through the walls. It's about sharing meals, stories, and experiences that enrich our lives and bring us closer together.

Making handmade cards, preparing meals, and organizing gatherings brings a sense of warmth and connection. These efforts create a community spirit that resonates deeply. Imagine the joy of seeing someone smile when they receive your card, or the laughter shared around a potluck dinner. These actions matter. They build bridges and strengthen bonds.

This book has shared numerous ideas for creating an atmosphere filled with love and joy. Whether it's exploring local holiday events or finding free activities, there's no shortage of ways to celebrate without financial strain. The world offers so much beauty and joy for those willing to seek it.

As you prepare for the holiday season, keep in mind that the greatest gift you can give is your presence. Show up for the people you love. Be there in times of joy and in times of sorrow. Your willingness to support others during the holidays speaks volumes.

Let's not forget the importance of self-care, especially during the busy holiday season. Amid the hustle and bustle, carve out time for yourself. Reflect on your experiences, savor the moments, and recharge your spirit. When you care for yourself, you're better equipped to care for others.

The spirit of Christmas is a call to action. It encourages us to take part in our communities, share our resources, and uplift one another. Every small effort counts, whether it's organizing a toy drive, volunteering at a shelter, or simply smiling at a stranger. Together, we can create a season filled with warmth, kindness, and understanding.

Embrace the lessons learned from this book. Carry them with you throughout the year, not just during the holiday season. Let the spirit of Christmas inspire you to cultivate love, gratitude, and kindness in your everyday life. The world needs more of these qualities, and each of us holds the power to spread them.

Reflect on what Christmas means to you. Let it shape your actions and intentions. Every act of kindness, every moment of laughter, every shared story contributes to the greater good. It's about building a legacy of love and connection that transcends time and space.

In the end, we all want to be seen and heard. The holiday season offers an opportunity to embrace our shared humanity. Let's celebrate our differences while finding common ground. Let's lift each other up, share our stories, and create a world where kindness reigns.

So as we close this chapter, remember the true essence of Christmas. It's not about what's under the tree, but the love and connections we share with one another. Embrace the spirit of giving, be present for your loved ones, and cherish every moment. The memories created during this season will last a lifetime, filling your heart with warmth and joy.

Now, as you head into this holiday season, carry these thoughts with you. Be a beacon of light and love in your community. Celebrate with all your heart, and remember that the magic of Christmas lives on in each of us. The journey doesn't end here; it continues as we strive to make the world a better place, one small act of kindness at a time.

| Page

Don't miss out!

Visit the website below and you can sign up to receive emails whenever Leroy M. Rhoades publishes a new book. There's no charge and no obligation.

https://books2read.com/r/B-A-EHBPC-UFDDF

BOOKS 2 READ

Connecting independent readers to independent writers.

Also by Leroy M. Rhoades